Esoteric Magic and the Cabala

Phillip Cooper

 Magickmeister

Esoteric Magic and the Cabala

Copyright © 2022 by Phillip Cooper

www.magickmeister.com

ISBN 978-1-7399019-7-4

First published in 2002 by Red Wheel/Weiser, LLC.

A CIP catalogue record for this book is available from the British Library.

Cooper, Phillip, 1955-

Esoteric magic and the cabala / Phillip Cooper.

Includes bibliographical references.

　　1.　Cabala. I. Title.

Cover design by Phillip Cooper

Preface

The study of Magic is much more than merely reading some books and lessons. A plethora of teachers and schools have material on the subject of the Tree of Life, and while some of this material is valuable, much of it is worthless when it comes to the question, "What the heck can you do with it?" In the practices prescribed in this book, you are called upon to make a drawing of the Tree of Life and asked to meditate upon the mystical-magical processes described in this book. The real study and work in Magic depends upon you *doing* the things called for in the books I write. Do not neglect these practices or just do them in passing, but put a great deal of effort and attention into them.

Also, begin to see how your magical studies can be applied to your daily life. Begin to *think* magical! That is, make your magical knowledge part of the way you see the world and the way you see yourself. As you learn to think magical, you will find that you experience a much greater reality than you ever anticipated. It is like putting on a new pair of eyeglasses—suddenly you see more, and you see more clearly.

Magic does not tell you how you should act. It does not give you sets of rules or commandments. But, as you begin to see things differently, as you think magical, you will begin to make your own determinations of how you should act, and what you should do in given circumstances. Magic places the responsibility for your life right on your own shoulders. But it also shows you that you have the power to make your life what you want it to be! Power and responsibility always go hand-in-hand, in Magic as in all things.

Table of Contents

Introduction

The techniques of Esoteric Magic differ from Practical Magic because the aim is different. You cannot mix the two, although the two paths can, and should, complement each other.

Esoteric or "High" Magic is the study of Magic in its own right. It involves self-development through inner work involving the workings of the universe and the understanding of how we, as individuals, fit into the greater scheme. Magic is a science—probably the greatest science of all—but unless truth is the goal, all will be in vain.

Up until now, no one has offered a truly realistic pattern of study. The established works are either emaciated in religious dogma or full of needless complexities designed to denigrate the student or based on superstitious concepts best left in the realms of pure fantasy. The magical lodges, to whom we are supposed to turn for enlightenment, are largely dominated by Golden Dawn techniques that have not advanced for over a hundred years.[1] Secret societies abound with their inevitable promise to reveal the secrets of Magic if you become an initiate. Becoming an initiate usually involves giving up your right of free choice in exchange for being the subject of some medieval pantomime. You may be asked to

---

[1] The Hermetic Order of the Golden Dawn was one of the most prestigious orders flourishing at the turn of the century. The London Temple of the Golden Dawn, named Isis-Urania, was founded on 1 March 1888. For years all went well with The Golden Dawn, and much magical work was done, but personality clashes and other factors led to quarrels, revolts, and schism, and by 1903 the original Order was split into various warring factions. Today there are several organizations whose teachings and practice are ultimately derived from The Golden Dawn, although few of them teach the whole system. It is true too, of course, that much of this system was not original: component parts of it can be found scattered through esoteric writings of a thousand years of European history. The great achievement of The Golden Dawn was to synthesize a coherent, logical system of Practical Magic out of the scattered remains of a tradition that had been largely broken up by fifteen hundred years of religious persecution.

bow to nonexistent secret chiefs and imaginary gods with unpronounceable names, and you may find that it is far easier to get in than it is to get out. There is even evidence to suggest that certain factions use drugs and hypnosis to ensure that you stay loyal.

The plan of action presented in this book is both positive and realistic. It is not a rehash of Golden Dawn or any other outmoded system. At no time are you presented with strange, mystical puzzles or veiled secrets— you are given all the facts in plain English. This book begins with first principles and extends through each chapter into a complete, workable plan of study. As a complete novice, you will find it easy to understand. As a long-suffering student, you will find it refreshing, stimulating, and free from confusion.

With this book, you begin the study of the Cabala and the Tree of Life. The Tree of Life is a part of the basic system of the West, or the Occident, called the Cabala. Cabala is the name of an esoteric science linked to Judaism, whose origins may be ancient dating back to biblical times, attempting to explain the creation and the deep basic truths of the physical cosmos as received by Moses from God on Mount Sinai (The word Cabala roughly means "to receive" in Hebrew).[2] Then again, its development may only go back as far as renaissance Jewish mysticism, which became widespread in the Middle Ages, (Spain and Southern France) its body of wisdom has since developed and transmuted over the centuries to become what it is today.

---

[2] Gnosticism is closely related to the Cabala, however, it differs from it with regard to one crucial idea—that of "the creation." The Gnostics hold that something in the creation process became distorted and some "evil" (Demiurge) inverted the whole of the process, and we as humans became trapped. As material beings, we are the physical hostage of the Gnostic Demiurge, creator and ruler of the tangible world, known also as Rex Mundi, the King of the World, represents everything temporal and illusory. I personally believe the paradigm of the Gnostic-Cabala to be correct. The study of Ophiel's book *The Art and Practice of Contacting the Demiurge* will reveal much to those who wish to pursue to line of investigation.

Not only are you going to study the Tree of Life, but you are going to learn to use it as a means of study. Soon you will begin to think of it as a filing system (or even a computer program) by which you classify your knowledge and observations into an interrelated whole.

Also, as your studies of Esoteric Magic continue, you will see how Magic becomes part of your entire life—not just a special compartment, a Sunday religion, a party dress—and everything in life is going to have new meanings for you. Your study of the Tree of Life will continue for as long as you are interested in Magic, so it is probably going to continue the rest of your life!

Taking Your First Steps in Esoteric Magic

This book is very special. Unlike many other courses of instruction, it presents the truth about Esoteric Magic and the Cabala and opens an individual path to the inner mysteries. In order to derive maximum benefit from this book, remember this single formula, which will serve as your guide to successful Magic:

$$Input = Output.$$

One of the most important rules of Magic is that you get out only in direct proportion to what you put in. By this I mean the quality of input, and not necessarily the time and money.

Magic—the Beginning

It is said that when God uttered his own name, creation began. The first act of real Magic was the creation. The only ingredient was the creator itself. Touch your body and you touch the material presence of the Logos (existence of God) as well as that of your ancestors. Grasp this truth with your heart rather than with your fallible human intelligence and you have taken your first step toward Real Magic.

Since all things are One Sentient being, it follows that everything is alive and aware. Stars, rocks, water, and air are living entities and, equally with animal life (including humankind), they are aspects of the Divine Totality. This knowledge permeates all created things. In humankind alone, it is suppressed by a pathologically over developed intellect that inhibits the vital intuitive and moral faculties governing the behavior of most life forms.

It is also said that humankind is made in the image of God, in other words *creative.* In order to create we must understand the way in which God (Universal Intelligence) acts, and use this as a guide.

The holy name of God, the Tetragram, is a four-lettered name: YHVH. Those with astute minds will immediately see the significance of this, for the name equates to the four elements. From a magical point of view, this makes profound sense and can be enacted out ritually. Consider the scheme. God causes power to flow by speaking his name—in other words, by channeling this power through the four cardinal points of the Magic Circle. It then finds its fruition in physical earth. To ritualize this is quite simple and extremely important.

Social Magic

The social magician feels that involvement with groups of similar thinkers will lead him or her forward. Nothing could be further from the truth. Social Magic may seem like a good idea until you look at the concept in depth.

Why is it that people feel the need to join groups? Perhaps it's the belief that there's safety in numbers, known as the "herd instinct." In a herd, the evolvement of the individual or the group is in the hands of the loudest voice. As everyone knows, the loudest is not necessarily the best. Quite often, esoteric groups (including covens and lodges) are convened around the wrong nucleus, so it naturally follows that if the nucleus is wrong then the entire structure is wrong.

Social Magic has little to offer any serious student, and while esoteric groups may be able to teach you something, at best they teach you what not to do. Before making contact with any group, you should ask the following questions:

1. What are the aims of this group? Are these realistic?

2. Do they offer enlightenment at a price? I do not simply mean money. Look at the cost in real terms.

3. Are there any demands on your freedom of choice?

4. Do they preach subservience to some entity, god, or secret chiefs?

5. Do they advocate sexual deviation? This includes anything from simple nudity to "Sex Magic."

If the answer is yes to any of these questions, then I urge you to avoid contact. All too often, innocent searchers have joined so-called magical groups only to find that they had been deceived. At least they were lucky enough to see that something was wrong and get out. Many never see the folly of social Magic and even become staunch supporters of such practice. Hearing the defensive arguments of such people makes me think "they doth protest too much."

Of course, as many have found out, it is always easier to get in these groups than it is to get out—and this can lead to much bigger problems. Adepts of Magic, using subtle techniques can be highly skilled in hypnosis (conversational hypnosis) and mind-control, and the controlling of large groups of people through fear-based psychosis. Most social Magic is simply harmless self-deception, but some groups will stop at nothing to prevent you from going your own way. It is disturbing that groups that preach freedom only allow you that freedom within the restrictions of their own system! You may well be on a path, but which path? Whose path? Is it truly yours, or is it someone else's? More to the point—where does it lead?

Trickery and the Master Occultist

If you have every watched the 1968 British horror movie, based on the 1934 novel of the same name by Dennis Wheatley *The Devil Rides*

Out, (known as *The Devil's Bride* in the United States).[1] There is a superb scene where the sinister Mr. Mocata (Charles Gray) comes to visit the house of Marie Eaton (Sarah Lawson) and subtly puts her under a hypnotic spell; Mocata is a ruthless magician who runs a cult of Devil-worshippers, where nobody ever gets to leave. Mr. Mocata has the grade of Ipsissimus 10=1, which make him a master adept corresponding to the Cabalistic Sephirah of Kether.[2] Wheatley interviewed Aleister Crowley while writing the book, whom he based Mr. Mocata's character on.

If you are a dedicated searcher, then you are bound to come in contact with others who can and will help. The old adage: "When the pupil is ready, a teacher will appear," is literally true, because the inner drive seeks answers and someone else may well have those answers. There is nothing wrong with having a teacher, provided that you first apply the aforementioned rules. There is nothing more pathetic than seeing otherwise sane and sensible individuals throwing caution to the wind in an effort to sit at the feet of some "master."

The Individual Path of Self-Initiation

The only realistic magical path is one of individual effort leading to the truth—anything less is pointless. However, you can learn from others and, in some instances, work with other people, provided that you do not give up individuality and freedom. In terms of our initial paradigm of "input = output," individual effort is the highest quality of input, and therefore the resulting output is bound to be ideal and more in keeping with your true path in life.

---

[1] Hammer Film Productions Ltd.
[2] Sephirot, meaning emanations, are the 10 spheres/emanations on the Cabalistic Tree of Life, through which the Negative Veils (Creator) reveals itself and continuously creates both the physical realm and the higher metaphysical realms. The term is alternatively transliterated into English Sephirot (Sephirah, singular).

You are an individual. There is no one else like you in existence, so it naturally follows that there is only one path to follow—your own. The path leads to your own truth concerning your real self and your relationship with the universe. No teacher can ever deliver you this truth, but a teacher can show you the way by giving you a realistic pattern of perfection based on universal truths—for example, laws that apply to everyone whatever their individual path may be. You have already been given one such law. It applies to everyone, and yet it allows total freedom of expression, for such is the nature of cosmic law and truth. Never treat your magical work as some sort of hobby or part-time interest that you fit in whenever you can spare a little time. If you do, the input = output law will yield disappointing results.

The Assumption of the God Forms

In order to work effective Magic, you must identify with the magician. You must be tricked over the line of disbelief by this cosmic thimble-rigger whose function is to dazzle you with his sleights into accepting that everything is possible. This is your first rung on the ladder of initiation.

The popularity of the tarot in divination sometimes obscures its function as a system of applied Magic.[3] A useful exercise is known as the "assumption of the god forms," but do not be put off by that expression. It is as easy as copying the style and mannerisms of your current role model. Daydreamers do this quite naturally. And most people are already acting roles imposed upon them by society and the mass-minded mold. This means recognizing that, potentially, nothing is beyond your power to

---

[3] By far the best esoteric tarot deck is the Rider-Waite as this uses good symbolism and has the advantage of the Minor Arcana cards containing pictures rather than "pips." Esoteric decks can be used for divination, meditation, and magical work and therefore offer better value.

achieve. The real test of achievement is the ability to be at ease with your true self and avoid seeing worldly values as anything but a dangerous illusion. If you do this, then nothing will ever dim the Magic in your eyes. And you will have learned for yourself the great secret.

Use your knowledge of the symbolism of The Magician, the second card of the Major Arcana, numbered 1, and try to identify with the character.

A young man stands in front of an altar. He is wearing a white and red cloak. In front of him lie four magical weapons: a Sword, a Wand, a Cup, and a Pentacle. A symbol of eternity hangs over his head. ∞ He holds a Wand in one raised hand and the other hand points down to the earth. These symbols represent the four control symbols for the four elements: Air, Fire, Water, and Earth. The Magician can make anything happen.

Study the picture on the morning of the New Moon. Concentrate on The Magician and become The Magician by identifying with his character and behavior. For the next fourteen days (until the Full Moon), think yourself into the character for at least five to ten minutes each day. In Magic, you choose your role. You are no longer one of life's bit players. The more you study the meaning of this card, the easier this role playing will become. After fourteen days, you will have completed the exercise. But do not mistake it for the Magic that is safe within your mind. It is only a mnemonic picture.

Discovery Magic, means recognizing the illusory nature of the material world. The real seat of learning and the channel for creative energy lies in the subconscious mind. This remarkable facet of our minds is inherent in each one of us, and its capabilities are enormous. It predates all spoken and written words. Images and actions are its language. It reads the heart and obeys the True Will. Languages see the world as objects and materials in space when it is really an illusion caused by a single, living process. The energy causing the process and creating the phantasmagoria you mistake for reality is the power that is harnessed both to accomplish Practical Magic and to delve into the mysteries of creation using Esoteric Magic.

Your Choice of Path

Magic is the art and science of understanding and using the vast potential of the subconscious mind. There are two branches to this science, each one dealing with the subconscious in different ways. It is important that the two are not confused.

In today's terminology we have "low" and "high" Magic. This is not a good description because it implies that one branch of Magic ("low") is trivial and therefore beneath consideration, which is not the case. A better classification is that of Practical Magic and Esoteric Magic. Practical Magic is wholly concerned with using the power of the subconscious to attain solid, physical results such as increased money supply, better health, or even a new home. In fact anything that enhances the lifestyle of an individual belongs to the realm of Practical Magic. On the other hand, Esoteric Magic is concerned with the study of Magic as a subject in its own right and also includes less tangible aims such as the discovery of inner truths and the understanding of the workings of creation.

Although this book is mostly concerned with Esoteric Magic, the basic principles lead naturally to practical studies of the magical arts because the same basic rules apply to both lines of study. However, it should always be remembered that, unless the would-be magician has learned the truth about the material world and, more important, learned how to control this, he or she is unlikely to make any real progress in esoteric matters. In magical terms the first real "initiation" is that of your ability to master the material illusion presented by life.

Your Relationship with the Universe

Our world was created by demonic (as opposed to angelic) intelligences to give themselves form and habitat outside the dream-time Eden from which they were ejected.[4] Humankind is the purposely made vehicle for the administration of malignant evil in the material realm. Humankind alone is genetically primed with what our ancestors called original sin, and the ruthless expunging of this inherent pollution is the first step in magical or mystical aspiration.

Demonic control is not confined to the ordinary unawakened man or woman but manifests as the Group Entity (or Egregores) of every corporate body.[5] States, churches, newspapers, committees, and charities as well as street gangs are directed by a demonic Group Entity that is neither human nor yet the combined personalities of the members. But is an identity that demands recognition and that uses the corporate image to conceal its true purpose—the domination of the material world by forces of undiluted and malignant evil.

But the process that creates this Vale of Tears, or *Lachrymal Mundi* (Tears of the World), in which war, famine, pestilence, and death reign supreme brings with it some angelic elements from the dream-time Eden. These occur as those rare virtues that some people share with animals and

---

[4] Common to all natural societies and was remembered in folktales, rituals, and art. Dream-time spirits created all things when bird and beast and humankind were one and death was but a dream. The dream-time spirits made the laws by which humans were required to live in harmony with the rest of Nature in order to thrive and eventually to return to the dream-time realm.

[5] Egregores are group mind entities. This is quite a loose term that is sometimes used to denote any group mind considered in the abstract, but it is more meaningful when applied to a well-defined magical entity deliberately created by a group of magicians. It also covers gods and goddesses, totems, or clan animals of tribes.

Nature, which, but for Luciferian pride, might raise humankind to the moral level and innocent state of those creatures so abused in psychopathic arrogance.

It is these rare angelic virtues in those of pure heart and noble spirit that offer the only glimmer of light in a world that Homo sapiens has turned into a materialistic demonocracy. Are you awake yet or do you still sleep?

Black Magic, White Magic, Which Is the Right Magic?

It surprises many beginners that the training for Black Magic and White Magic is exactly the same. A trained adept can use the power for anything. The choice is left entirely to the individual concerned. After many years of training, most adepts are not susceptible to guilt feelings induced by church, state, and society. They understand that these three phantoms of illusion separate you from reality and Magic. To a magician, the color black means "creation made manifest," or "idea turned into fact." An artist or inventor will have an idea, a pure thought. They will then paint or built it. Black represents the finished, physical article. Therefore, true Black Magic is concerned with the physical result as opposed to the pure thought, or spiritual side, which is White Magic.

Esoteric Magic

Looking beyond the obvious is what Esoteric Magic is all about. It is the truth that you seek, and you will rapidly learn that the apparent facts are not always true, so it becomes folly to use these as a basis for belief. The equation that successfully explains your true relationship to life-energy is:

$$You = Your\ Belief\ Patterns = Energy$$

This apparently simple statement explains all of life's problems and also gives you the key to a vast reserve of power.

You

You have a subconscious mind that is capable of great things, miraculous things. How does it work? Perhaps the best way to understand the subconscious is by equating it to a vast computer. First, it makes no moral judgments; it simply acts on instructions and seeks to carry these out to the letter. If you consider the fact that the same computer can run an entire factory or detonate a hydrogen bomb, you will soon grasp the idea.

Your subconscious mind is nothing less than a tool to be used to create whatever you wish. The problem is that people have lost sight of this simple truth by allowing others, less informed, priests and/or leaders to think for them.

Your Belief Patterns

Belief alone makes your world what it is. You have been conditioned to believe in illusion. Let me teach you to believe in reality.

Regardless of other people, your belief and image patterns will cause your subconscious mind to bring into your life all manner of physical facts, which directly relate to these beliefs. This is the basis on which scientific Magic becomes a reality. Put quite simply, *thoughts produce things,* or looked at another way; every dominant thought causes an effect. Note that I specify *dominant* thoughts, for if every fleeting thought had power, life would indeed be a far greater problem that it is at present.

With any computer, the type of program used will determine how it functions. Exactly the same happens with your subconscious mind. Given a program (belief), it will act on it without hesitation. Now can you see why things go wrong in your life? The problems are created not by external forces, fate, God's will, or even curses—they are caused by incorrect programming (wrong beliefs).

Your subconscious mind is capable of many things. In the first instance, it can and does affect the physical side of life through beliefs. It is impossible to overestimate the power of the subconscious mind. Not only will it carry out every command you give it but it will also answer all questions. It is this latter fact that we make use of in Esoteric Magic.

Energy

Your ability to manipulate energy patterns extends to all physical matter, from the regeneration of body tissues to causing something physical in response to your desires. Your beliefs act as instructions to your subconscious mind, so obviously you will cause the physical world to react according to these beliefs. By changing beliefs, your future is in your own hands, for you are bound to change the future.

Magic concedes that the very rocks have no solidity other than the illusion created by pure energy dancing in a particular pattern. Throughout history, the finest craftspeople have been those who commune with the energy that gives the illusion of tactile reality to metal, stone, wood, textiles, and everything else. A master craftsperson is therefore a true magician. This is why you should familiarize yourself with basic crafts until you feel and respond to the soul of the tools and materials. In Magic, we seek to dispel the material illusion sufficiently to experience the Magic within.

You have at your disposal vast reserves of power. Look at the power of Nature, in particular the enormous energy at work in the heavens. The Sun is a prime example. It burns billions of tons of its own fuel every day, yet it never gets cooler.[6] Imagine if you could harness this amount of force for only one second. There is a vast amount of energy in the universe, and it is not beyond your reach. Far from it. It is part of your existence, and your subconscious mind has access to this power. Your subconscious mind deals with energy; it knows every conceivable combination, and it knows how to use these to alter circumstances according to whatever instructions are given to it. You can rest assured that in the creative scheme of life there will never be a lack of energy. If it ever did dry up, then the universe as we know it would be truly inert and lifeless.

Universal Energy is not chaotic; it conforms to very precise laws. If it were truly chaotic, then life would be impossible. Cabbage seeds would turn into diamonds. But this cannot happen. A cabbage is always a cabbage. Its structure is determined by precise laws. How would you perform a miracle and change a cabbage into a diamond? The answer lies in changing the energy pattern, not by invoking chaos (or the gods). Although you do not, as yet, have the knowledge to do this, it is not beyond the realm of possibility. After all, a very talented man changed water into wine by knowing about, and applying, the law of transmutation.[7]

Your subconscious mind knows every pattern of energy inexistence, and it also has the ability to change these. When given an instruction, in the form of a belief, it first locates the target, recognizes its energy pattern, and then proceeds to change it so that it conforms to the new instruction.

---

[6] Damon T Berry does a tremendous job of explaining the reality of navigating the stars, the Sun/stars as portals and black holes and certain aspects of Earth's hidden history, etc. Damon T Berry's *The Knowledge of the Forever Time.*

[7] "When the ruler of the feast had tasted the water that was made wine, and knew not whence it was: (but the servants which drew the water knew.)" John 2:9 from the King James version.

In order to understand the nature and workings of this energy, we must find some means of dividing it into convenient units. There are several systems that attempt to do this. The best by far is the Cabalistic Tree of Life. This incredible system helps us categorize energy—and indeed everything else—in life.

The Magical Trident

We gain access to the knowledge and power of the subconscious mind through:

1. The mind.
2. The emotions.
3. The imagination.

These are the points of the magical trident. The trident's handle equates to the will. The use of these three approaches will be discussed in detail later on, but briefly, to activate the subconscious, first there has to be an intention. This is then directed into subconscious levels through any or all of these three access points. Sustained will is equivalent to belief, and belief always gets results.

Cause and Effect

All dominant thoughts or beliefs that exist in your subconscious mind are causing things to happen. These may be good or bad and may be completely unknown to your conscious mind. It is very easy to blame external forces or suppressed demons. In the same way, it is easy to credit some beneficial angel if and when something pleasant happens, but the plain truth is that you are causing these things to happen, and every cause must have an effect.

You may, by free choice, cause things to happen by using this same law. In this case all that needs to be done is to give your subconscious mind a new instruction in a way it can understand. The techniques used to do this are classified as Magic. Cause and effect is therefore a just and correct law, for it seeks to give to each individual that which he or she conceives.

All things—animate and inanimate, abstract and concrete—are one substance. Everything came from the one source therefore everything contains life and is linked together. If you touch a spider's web, the vibration resonates through the web. If you are on the web, you feel the vibrations. To touch the web of life is to send out a message to everything in creation. To send out a thought is to vibrate the web of life that connects every living creature and life energy through the laws of cause and effect. Like attracts like, and cause is always matched by effect. A sustained thought always reaches everything in creation that is in keeping with that thought, and by virtue of this fact so do cosmic energy and Universal Intelligence respond to your thoughts. Effort is therefore rewarded by the response of energy; every cause must have an effect.

Resolve here and now to make use of the law of cause and effect by concentrating on those things that you truly wish to have. Be positive. Do not dwell on problems; only seek their solution, and do not restrict your thoughts to that which seems obvious. Raise your sights and your thinking above the obvious and life energies will respond to this new mode of thinking. Be bold, be optimistic, be enthusiastic, and dwell on what you desire. Yours thoughts have an effect on invisible levels of life beyond the obvious.

Symbolism and the Subconscious

Having covered some of the basic truths of life, let us now start to build a bridge between conscious and subconscious levels.

The language of the subconscious is symbolism. The subconscious does not understand English or indeed any other language; it only understands symbols. There are many types of symbols. For now we will consider the two main types: abstract and personal.

Abstract Symbols

Abstract symbols such as the Encircled Cross below are highly potent forms that instantly convey a mass of useful information. The more you think about them, the more information they will give you. This information comes directly from your memory—in other words, your subconscious mind. By using magical symbols, you can obtain magical information in great depth, because your subconscious has no limits. It is also important to remember that you use a symbol; you do not make it an object of worship or consider it to be holy. By all means, treat symbols with respect, but *never* turn them into idols.

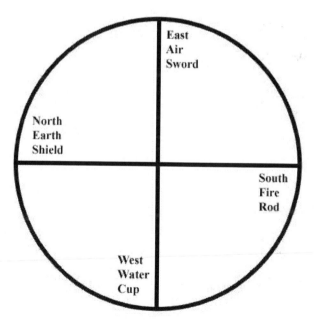

Figure 1. The Encircled Cross.

Personal Symbols

Unlike the former personal, or telesmatic, symbols are personifications of some desirable quality or power. An archangel or planetary deity is an example of this type of symbol. While personal symbols are useful in Magic, they must be kept in perspective. Always remember that they are *symbols;* they do not exist other than as symbols within the imagination of the practitioner. The danger with this type of symbol is that the practitioner starts to believe in the symbol as a reality in its own right. If man and woman build powerful telesmatic images (symbols) of the worst kind, the law of cause and effect will bring a wicked harvest. Until the image of God is changed, humankind will continue to suffer through its own beliefs. The message is simple: Do not use telesmatic images unless you can build them with desirable qualities.

The Master Symbol: The Encircled Cross

It is unfortunate that the present trend leads the eager neophyte toward the use of the Pentagram and Hexagram. The correct procedure is to start with the Encircled Cross, which, apart from being the master symbol, is the symbol from which all others emanate. As a basis for magical development there is no other that is better.

The Encircled Cross is the real Magic Circle in which you function on inner levels. Before you can use it successfully, you have to understand it. The old idea of the magician standing within the protective Magic Circle while fighting off demons is incorrect. First, there are no such things as demons (telesmatic images that epitomize qualities). Second, and more to the point, the circle is valueless unless it is built in the mind. Painting a circle on the floor (or buying one in cheap plastic) is simply pointless unless you wish to regress to the dark ages.

This symbol, together with a few of its main attributions, is given in figure 1 (see page 19). Do not be put off by its simplicity. This symbol, if used correctly, can develop into a highly complex and all-embracing magical system. Get to know it.

The Perfection of Magic

Read through this chapter at least once a day and think carefully about the ideas contained herein. These ideas may defy convention and perhaps seem oversimplified, but they are correct.

Here is another magical formula:

$$Peace = Power$$

It is almost impossible to perform a magical act if your mind is filled with everyday thoughts and stress. I cannot emphasize the importance of the peace = power equation too strongly. Access to the subconscious is restricted in proportion to activity. The high point of any ritual is reached in a state of absolute calm, for real power lies within the secret, silent center within us. The antics of those would-be magicians who insist on cavorting around the temple are in direct opposition to the truth. You do not have to work yourself up into a frenzy to raise power, quite the reverse. You must slow down.

Relaxation, especially pre-ritual relaxation, is vital to your success. Spend some time each day learning how to relax the body and mind. There are many techniques that assist relaxation.

Regular practice with the Encircled Cross will help build a bridge between you and your subconscious mind. Without this bridge, contact with this seat of power is strictly limited, so practice often.

You will need a candle and some general incense or joss sticks for this exercise. Enter your temple or place of work (see pp. 23-25), burn some incense, and sit quietly and relax while clearing away all thoughts of everyday matters. After a suitable period, begin to contemplate the idea of peace = power. Let the words *tranquility, calm, stillness,* and *silence* come into your mind as you let go and deeply relax. Take your time and allow inner peace to take the place of normal activity. Silent stillness is the key to real power and truth and is therefore well worth the time spent in discovering it.

When you have reached a satisfactory state of calm, light the altar candle, which now symbolizes this inner peace and eternal source of power. Contemplate the idea of using a candle in this way. Symbolism is very important in Magic, for symbols and symbolic acts speak volumes to your subconscious mind.

Now imagine that you are taking a journey into inner space. You get smaller and smaller until you can see the individual cells within your body. Continue getting smaller until you can see molecules, atoms, the parts of an atom, and so on, until you can go no farther. At this point you have reached the silent center of power. Now imagine a point of light forming and getting larger and brighter. Move your attention to your heart area and imagine that this light emanates from your heart. It grows and continues to get brighter until it radiates all through your body.

Do not let logical thinking get in the way; simply use your imagination without trying to be rational, critical, or analytical. Logic, as you will discover, has only a limited part to play in magical working. I should also mention that it is not necessary that you strain to visualize. If you can visualize, well and good. If not, then do not try to sustain vivid pictures; instead, simply let the mind consider and reflect on each idea in the same way that you do this naturally in everyday matters.

In the next part of the exercise, you will erect the true Magic Circle, the Encircled Cross, within your mind. It is quite simple. Start by imagining that a shaft of light proceeds from your heart to some convenient point immediately in front of you. This is magical east. Imagine the same thing happening to your right. This is magical south. Next, see a similar beam of light go from your heart to a similar distance behind you. This is magical west. Finally, complete the cosmic cross by imagining a beam of light going out to your left. This is magical north.

Starting from magical east, imagine a circle of light connecting each of these four points in turn. You now have a complete Encircled Cross, or Magic Circle. Contemplate this symbol for a while, allowing ideas and impressions to arise in your mind. In conclusion, reverse the procedure, finally allowing the light to disappear within your heart. Extinguish the candle and return to normal.

Keep a magical notebook in which you record any important thoughts, feelings, experiences, and ideas. No need for long-winded essays; brief notes will suffice. These notes will be extremely useful at some future date. In the meantime, practice this exercise often—it is the first step in building a powerful magical system that is truly your own.

The Magical Temple

Privacy is a prerequisite to successful magical practice. You simply cannot achieve the correct state of mind if you are constantly subjected to distractions and noise. You must have somewhere to work that is removed from everyday life. Circumstances will dictate where it will be, depending on how much space is available. In the final analysis, you must decide on the type of temple you need. Below are a few suggestions for temples and equipment.

Permanent Temple

A spare room is ideal. Put a lock on the door and curtain any windows in the interest of security and secrecy. In all cases, keep your magical work and your temple secret. There are still enough ignorant bigots in existence who will try to make life uncomfortable, so do not take risks.

Temporary Temple

If there is no permanent free space, then use whatever means you have in hand. A little ingenuity works wonders. Often you can adapt a bedroom or even the garden shed. Take your time, think things through, and work out a suitable compromise. Again, security and privacy are essential—either put a lock on the door, invent some suitable excuse to keep people away, or simply insist on privacy. You cannot fully concentrate on what you are doing if you are in constant fear of someone disturbing you.

Temple Equipment

A temple, in essence, is nothing more than a workroom. You only need useful equipment in a workroom. The golden rule with equipment is do not bring it into your temple unless you have a good reason for doing so. In addition, make certain that you fully understand its purpose. Failure to do this often results in temples that resemble junk shops rather than well-ordered places of work.

You will need an altar. This is simply a work surface. It can be an elaborate double cube or simply a small cupboard or coffee table. The choice is yours. Altar cloths are quite useful, as they bring color into a ritual. An incense burner, candles, and candle holders are also basic equipment. The choice of colors, shapes, and sizes is again a matter of choice. Again, think carefully before you decide, and do not be swayed by what the books say—make up your own mind. Robes are optional and not essential in the early stages. It is usually better to spend time perfecting your magical system in as simple a way as possible. Ideas about robes and so forth will gradually occur with the passage of time and in proportion to experience.

Finally, a magical temple is not a place of worship. It is, if you like, simply a psychic laboratory, where you learn about your inherent power and also test out your ideas. By all means treat it with respect and make it a special place, but please do not dedicate it to the gods. Let science take the place of superstition.

The Cosmic Plan, the Encircled Cross, and the Cosmic Sphere

The mysteries and secrets of real Magic lie in the understanding of the subconscious mind. You give the subconscious mind an instruction either directly (as in a correctly performed ritual or act of Magic) or inadvertently (through beliefs, whether they be correct or wrong). The subconscious mind will always carry out this direction, no matter what the facts appear to be. This incredible part of yourself is totally limitless, creative, and all-knowing. How? To touch the universal web of life is to cause vibration. Every cause has an effect, so to send out a thought vibrates the web of life that connects everything, because all things are one sentient being.

Subconscious—Universal Energy and Universal Intelligence

The fact that Universal Energy is so precise in its action suggests that there is an intelligence behind it. This Universal Intelligence is responsible for creation as we know it, for it shapes inert matter into recognizable, physical objects and gives them life. This creative process is free-flowing and unrestricted. Creation gives life and creates freely; it does not seek to restrict, destroy, or enforce its will. It simply is and as such, it can only be beneficial.

As a human being, you have a very special place in the creative scheme, for you also have the capacity to create. By believing this to be true, you cause it to be true. You have the power to create, and you can, and do, create using the same system operating in the universe. Your subconscious mind uses Universal Energy and manipulates its patterns on demand. In addition, being part of the creative process, it is a vital part of Universal Intelligence. It is nothing less than the God within having access to all aspects of creation and the wonders of life's mysteries. To say that you have a hotline to God is therefore true. You are far greater than you believe yourself to be, and you really do have the power to create whatever you wish, because there are no limits except those you accept yourself.

Subconscious—Universal Mind

Consider the very simple fact that you as an individual have two minds. The first is your conscious mind, the part of you that thinks. You use it all the time to observe, to evaluate. The other mind is your subconscious mind. This is not far removed or deeply hidden, nor does it take a great deal of skill to use. It has two functions. First, it looks after all the automatic functions in your body (such as breathing, heartbeat, tissue regeneration, growth of hair). The second function is to store information in your memory and to act according to your wishes.

You have the capacity to be whatever you want, to have whatever you desire. You are in contact with the whole of creation. Everyone has a subconscious mind with exactly the same capacity for handling power or communicating over vast distances. If you put all of these minds together—wherever they may be, either on this planet or any other in the vastness of creation—you have a Universal Mind. Through this Universal Mind you are able to draw on all the thinking that has gone before, for all memories are stored within.

Perhaps you have read or heard of the great symbolic library of knowledge called the Akashic Records. According to ancient mystical doctrines, the name stems from the Sanskrit word *akasha*, meaning "primary substance," or that out of which all things are formed. Therefore, we can say that the Akashic Records are the indelible and eternal records of the Universal Mind, containing all knowledge of the past, present, and future. Of course, these are not materially written accounts, but rather they are an expression of the totality of universal wisdom.

It is easy to see that the Akashic Record is simply another way of expressing the fact that, through the universal linkage of minds, nothing is ever forgotten. This record can be read literally like a book. Of course it must be done through your own subconscious mind using sensible techniques, but it is there to be explored by anyone who takes the time and trouble to look in the right way. In truth we are all linked together through this mind, and we have the ability to span the vastness of time and explore the enormous reserves of knowledge and power that the Universal Mind contains.

The entire scheme is represented by the triangle in figure 2. Here, the triangle is being used to represent an idea—it is a symbol. Study it carefully.

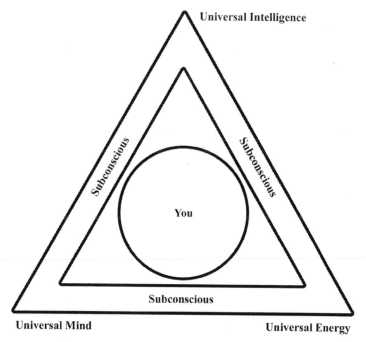

Figure 2. The Universal Triangle.

Symbols

The key to the subconscious, especially from a magical point of view, lies in the use of symbols. Any valid symbol acts as a link between you and this powerful part of your mind. Symbols are the keys that unlock the door to power and knowledge if used correctly. Let us now explore a single symbol and see where it leads.

The Encircled Cross

Leaving aside Pentagrams, Hexagrams, and other highly dubious ancient designs of guaranteed efficacy, look at the master symbol, the Encircled Cross (see page 32). All other symbols are contained in this symbol, thereby making it a fitting starting point for your search.

There are three ways in which you can examine any symbol:

1. Think about it on a conscious level.
2. Contemplate the symbol.
3. Meditate on the symbol.

Conscious thought only deals with the obvious, but it does have its uses. So, taking the Encircled Cross as a starting point, let us see what obvious facts come to light.

There is a central point from which radiate four arms, and the whole is surrounded by a circle. The angle between the arms is ninety degrees, and there are four quadrants. This appears to sum up the design and does not reveal any profound truths or useful information. Now let us take things a stage further using contemplation.

As this is a universal symbol, you ought to be able to relate this to life. The number four brings to mind:

*   The four points of the compass (north, east, south, and west).

- The four seasons (winter, spring, summer, and autumn.
- The four periods of each day (dawn, noon, dusk, and midnight).
- The four suits of the tarot (Swords, Wands, Cups, and Pentacles).
- The four phases of the Moon (New Moon, First Quarter, Full Moon, and Last Quarter).
- The Four Elements (Air, Fire, Water, and Earth).
- The four fundamental forces that govern the universe (electromagnetism, strong nuclear force, weak nuclear force, and gravity).
- The fourfold descriptive division of matter (space, time, mass, and energy.
- The Tetragram, the fourfold name of the Hebrew God (YHVH) (pronounced Yod-Heh-Vav-Heh).[1]
- The four magical weapons (Sword, Rod, Cup, and Shield).

There are many more fourfold attributions, however, let us now take matters a little further using mediation.

Take the symbol and think *at* and *with* it. First, think about the list of previous attributions and try to relate these to the symbol. Clearly, the points on the circumference of the Encircled Cross resemble the points of a compass (north, east, south, and west). Now, fit the four periods of the day (dawn, noon, dusk, and midnight) on the Encircled Cross. There is a connection between the rising Sun at dawn and east, so dawn equates to the eastern point on the circumference. It naturally follows that as the Sun is at its zenith at noon and is therefore giving out maximum heat, so noon must equate to the south point. The Sun sets at dusk in the west, leaving the darkness of midnight to the north. A similar exercise can be done with the four seasons. Try this for yourself.

---

[1] A more initiated explanation of this is given in the following book: Ophiel, *The Art and Practice of the Occult* (York Beach, ME: Samuel Weiser, 1976), p. 38.

Direction: North
Season: Winter
Period of Day: Midnight
Tarot Suit: Pentacles
Moon Phase: Last Quarter
Element: Earth
Fundamental Force: Gravity
Matter: Mass
Tetragram: Heh
Magical Weapon: Shield

Direction: East
Season: Spring
Period of Day: Dawn
Tarot Suit: Swords
Moon Phase: New Moon
Element: Air
Fundamental Force: Weak
Nuclear Force
Matter: Space
Tetragram: Yod
Magical Weapon: Sword

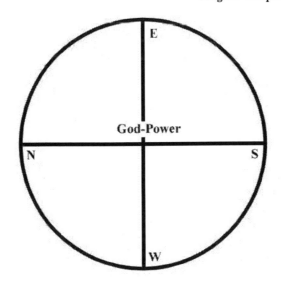

Direction: West
Season: Autumn
Period of Day: Dusk
Tarot Suit: Cups
Moon Phase: Full Moon
Element: Water
Fundamental Force: Electromagnetism
Matter: Time
Tetragram: Vav
Magical Weapon: Cup

Direction: South
Season: Summer
Period of Day: Noon
Tarot Suit: Wands
Moon Phase: First Quarter
Element: Fire
Fundamental Force: Strong Nuclear
Force
Matter: Energy
Tetragram: Heh
Magical Weapon: Rod

Figure 3. The Encircled Cross with Correspondences.

The Four Elements of the Encircled Cross

In Magic, you will find many references to the number four, from the Tetragram (four-lettered name of God) to the four worlds of the Cabalist to the enigmatic four elements of the wise. It is said that creation began when God uttered his name (the Tetragram: YHVH). The fourfold name created all. The obvious interpretation of this is that everything in creation contains the four elements, and therefore, the elements rule all that exists. The scheme is easily explained by the symbol. If the central point is taken to represent God beginning creation, power then radiated out in four distinct directions (The Caltrop of Chaos: the arms of the cross), finally creating all that is and ever will be (circle). The points at which the arms join the circle are termed the cardinal points, and at each point you have an element. The correct placing of these elements is given in figure 3 (see page 32).

You now have four points around the circle at which you can group together, or categorize, everything in existence, each point being ruled by an element. Obviously, it would take more than a single human life to produce any in depth list of physical objects and events that equate to the elements. This, in any case, is not necessary. All that needs to be understood is that vast groups of correspondences do indeed relate to each point and its ruling element. Also, when you stand within your symbolic Encircled Cross, you are automatically in touch with everything in creation, grouped under four cardinal points and their ruling elements.

So far, you have taken the symbol and looked out at the world, now you will view the symbol from a different angle—looking in. Look at the Encircled Cross in light of what has been said about the God-center radiating outward. Each arm of the cross represents a path. Naturally, this is two-way. If you now remember that your own center, or God within, is your subconscious mind, the symbol starts to reveal its power in practical terms. The relationship of your subconscious mind to God and Universal

Energy has already been discussed. Let us take the same idea and equate it to the Encircled Cross symbol.

The Center of the Encircled Cross

This center point equates to God-power, either universally or internally through your subconscious mind. It is your seat of power, through which you create by linking into God and power. From this center radiate four paths that connect to everyday life. That final connection is named a cardinal point and equates to the element.

The Paths of the Encircled Cross

Center and circumference are connected by four paths, and each path works in two ways. First, you can direct the power contained in the center along the path in order to affect physical changes. Second, you can use a physical object as an object of contemplation or meditation with a view toward tracking back along a path in order to discover the inner truth behind this object. In the latter method various objects and ideas corresponding to the nature of the energy being contemplated are used in ritual situations to act as a focus for the mind, which is then stimulated by their presence.

In dealing with the elements, you are faced with a profusion of choices as to which belongs where on the circle. To avoid having to make long lists of probabilities, it would be far better if you could epitomize each element and all that is ruled by this power by the use of a symbol. The idea being that one symbol would then represent an element in totality. Fortunately, this is not as difficult as you may suppose.

The Four Weapons of the Encircled Cross

Ancient tradition furnishes four valid symbols. These are Sword, Wand, Cup, and Shield. They are correctly placed as in figure 3 (see page

32). Each symbol, like the paths, can be used in two ways: in and out. For instance, the Sword can be used to direct the energy of Air or it can be used as a symbol for contemplation or meditation in order to track back to central truth. It should be stated that a physical representation of each weapon is not necessary at this stage. It is far more important to work with the symbol in the mind first. It's ridiculous to purchase a so-called Magic Sword in the hope that it will in itself cause great things to happen. It is the inner realization that matters, for without these, a physical Sword is useless. The same applies to any piece of magical equipment. First you work with the idea, gradually building up inner awareness so that when you do acquire a ritual item you will have a personal relationship with it. This modus operandi should also be applied to the other three magical weapons—the Rod, Cup, and Shield. I will say more about these in subsequent chapters.

The Doctrine of Correspondences

The grouping together of similar ideas and physical items is a valuable magical technique that needs examination. You have probably heard of lists of correspondences or seen these printed in books. Aleister Crowley's 777 was an attempt to categorize certain items and fit them to the Tree of Life.[2] By far the oldest idea is the speculation that everything in creation is ruled by the planets. In actual fact, the planets do not, as such, rule anything. This is an unfortunate choice of words. It would be more correct to state that there is a similarity between the name of a planetary energy and a physical fact. For example: Gold is ruled by the Sun. Here, the nature of the mental is similar to the nature of the planet. There is an affinity between the two.

---

[2] Aleister Crowley, *777 & Other Qabalistic Writings.* (York Beach, ME: Samuel Weiser, 1970).

There is a mistaken idea that if you bring together a few items that correspond to a particular planet, this, by itself, will attract the supposed power of the planet. This is not strictly true. While it can be argued that these materials may well vibrate at the same frequency or, in some cases, may even appear to emit energy, the gathering together of sympathetic materials will not in itself cause energy to flow. For instance, the gathering together of gold, sunflower seeds, frankincense, and a Hexagram in some ritual situation will do absolutely nothing. You are the only thing that causes power to flow. Never forget that items used ritually are not magical—they are simply concentration aids.

Your Encircled Cross is the real Magic Circle in which you symbolically stand during magical work. Up until now, it is just a symbolic circle. To make it usable, you have to relate it to life and the universe. The doctrine of correspondences will serve you well. If the Encircled Cross embraces everything in creation, then all things must relate to the symbol. In fact this is so.

The Encircled Cross
Becomes the Cosmic Sphere

Up until now, your Encircled Cross has been two-dimensional; it has been a flat representation of a three-dimensional reality. Let us now move away from flat circles into the idea of Cosmic Spheres. To do this you have to extend the Encircled Cross in this way.

Imagine two more radii emerging from the center. One goes vertically up, one vertically down. These are now encompassed by two more circles, giving the three rings of Cosmos. To aid visualization, these are shown in figure 4 (see page 37).

You now have a total of one center, three rings, and six nodal points. To make your cosmic scheme complete, you need attributions for the upper and lower points. With the elements, you are dealing with the expression and subsequent manifestation of power in four distinct ways. The upper and lower points equate to supply and demand. Looking up, you find God, or the All-Father, who supplies power. The All-Father gives out and is therefore positive. The lowermost point is obviously the reverse and so equates to Mother Nature, or Earth-Mother. She is receptive to power and is therefore negative. The word "negative" is not meant

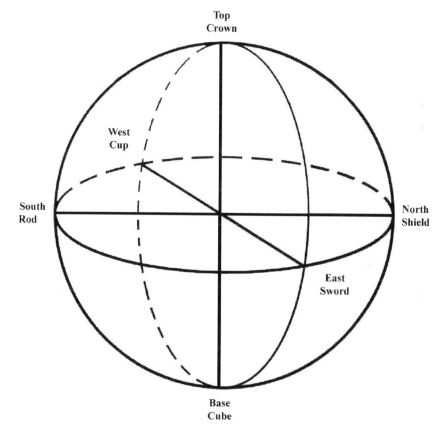

Figure 4. The Cosmic Sphere.

in any derogatory sense. Naturally, there is a path from the center to each point that works both ways once more, and there is also a symbol. The upper point is symbolized by a Crown and the lower is represented by a Cube.

You now have a complete three-dimensional Cosmic Sphere that has a central point of power and a periphery that encompasses everything in creation. The simple Encircled Cross has now become a Cosmic Sphere; all that remains is to individualize it. This is done by patient practice, including in it only those ideas that are valid and true for you.

Symbolism, the Four Elements, and the Four Magical Weapons

As a student of Magic, you could be excused for thinking that it will take years to sort out the confusion and contradictions that now exist in modern esoterics. Years of tortured study need not be necessary, provided that there is a plan of action using valid symbolism. The entire process can be equated to learning a language. The hard way is to buy heaps of books and then, all by yourself, try to make some sense out of it all. The easier way is to find a teacher or enroll in a course that helps you understand the subject by taking you through successive stages, from first principles until you gain proficiency. So it is with Magic. You have to start from basic principles, using a sensible plan of action. This takes time, but it is well worth the effort in terms of real understanding and self-advancement.

Symbols in Your Plan of Action

Magic works because of your inherent ability to use the power and knowledge contained within the subconscious mind. In order to contact this powerful part of yourself, you have to converse with it in a language that you, and it, can understand.

The only language that gets results is that of symbolism. Time and time again you will see symbols being abused, so in order to avoid time-wasting practices, let us look at symbols in a realistic light.

There are three types of symbols:

1.   Abstract: Usually geometric shapes such as the Pentagram, Hexagram, and the Encircled Cross, together with circle, square, triangle, and so forth.

2.   Personalized: Gods, archangels, angels, spirits, demons—in fact any tangible being of humanoid form, built up over centuries of adoration and/or sacrifice which, can be brought out of your subconscious as a personalized energy.

3.   Physical: All magical equipment, such as weapons, altar, candles, and even the temple itself.

The use of abstract, geometric symbols is vital in any magical system and they are meant to be worked with on inner levels of awareness in order to gain subconscious response.

There are numerous personalized symbols, ranging from the Christian God to the lowliest of spirits. Never make the mistake of presuming that these things exist as living entities—they do not! A symbol, whatever its nature, acts as an interchange between you and the type of energy that you are seeking to contact, be this for direct use or for the purpose of acquiring knowledge. These symbols do have a use if they are treated sensibly. All too often, however, they are not!

Personalized symbols, or telesmatic images as they are known, do have a use in the scheme of things. For instance, if you wish to approach a certain type of energy, let us say the element of Air, I think you will agree that it is difficult to converse with its symbol, the Sword. If, however, you imagine that there is some form of intelligence behind this element (which there is), it is far easier to deal with this in human terms—in other words build up the image of a being with whom you can converse. The other approach is to use some of the more sensible telesmatics such as the Cabalistic archangels. Much is to be gained from this technique, provided that you do not credit these imaginary beings with power over you. This is folly of the worst kind because whatever you build into a symbol, either abstract, personalized, or physical, is bound to have an effect on your subconscious mind and will therefore manifest itself in the physical world. If you must work with telesmatic images, then do so in the light of common sense by attributing only the most desirable qualities to each image.

In Magic, much use is made of physical objects, and this is valid provided that you again apply common sense. All too often, the would-be magician rushes out to buy some essential piece of ritual paraphernalia in the hope that this will entice power to flow. Nothing could be farther from the truth, so we will look at this aspect of Magic in some detail.

Take, for instance, the idea of a Magical Sword. Before you purchase one, or, if you are really talented, make one yourself, stop and think. What use does this have; what does it represent; and what are you going to do with it? The magical law is that all starts with thought, and so it is with physical symbols. Think first, then act. Failure to do this will result in lack of contact and perhaps needless expense.

We create with the subconscious mind using the four channels of creative power, so it naturally follows that to understand these channels is to give ourselves more control over this power. This is done by using a language that the subconscious mind understands—the language of symbolism.

The aim of the true magician is to link within the self the greater and lesser natures. To do this, many have used symbolic weapons to bridge the gap between physicality and mentality. The four principle weapons are symbolic of the elements: Air, Fire, Water, and Earth. The symbols for the four elements are Sword, Rod (or Wand), Cup (or Chalice), and Shield.

The Sword (Air)

The Sword represents the creative will and intelligence; it represents the ability to conceive an idea and bring it to reality in action.

The first mistake is to presume that a physical Sword contains power—it does not! You will read of elaborate ceremonies, in which the magician consecrates his or her Sword and, this is valid up to a point, but what is in fact happening is the concentration and dedication applied to the ritual is focusing the mind of the magician along certain lines, in this case the Sword. To a certain extent this is bound to get some subconscious response, but in this day and age these techniques are unnecessary. Far better to update the procedure in the light of sound practice and common sense. There are several techniques that are easy to follow and quite effective. First, you can work from a purely conscious level by thinking about a magical Sword. If you were to have one, what would be its shape, its size? What would the handle look like? Would it be jeweled and ornate? Think about it and make drawings until you are certain that this is your Sword. Do not accept the designs given in various textbooks and grimoires, for to do this is to defeat the whole object of the exercise. Look for your Sword and try to establish your contact with the element of Air. Use your imagination. Your subconscious mind does not understand the English language; it works with symbols and pictures that are used imaginatively. The more you imagine, the better the picture and, the more cooperation you will get from your subconscious.

Use this imaginary picture to take you further and further towards your own power. There are many techniques; here is just one: Working within your Magic Circle of four elements, face the appropriate cardinal point (in this case east) and use your imagination to see a yellow doorway (yellow being the color of Air). Pass through this door and see an altar. Your Sword is on this altar. Look around to see if anything else is apparent, perhaps a landscape or people. Pick up the magical Sword and feel the air blowing around you. You are in control; you are directing the element of Air. Allow impressions to arise from your subconscious mind. When you have finished, replace the Magic Sword. Go back through the door, close the door and, return to normal. Close down the temple and write up any important points for future reference.

Techniques like this will go a long way in helping you to understand the element of Air and the Magical Sword as it applies to you. You do not have to use this technique exactly as described. Be flexible and vary it to suit yourself. You have to relate the element of Air to Earth life and, this is best done by thinking about the Sword—what it does and how it could be used. Look at everyday life and find Swords and Sword-like situations. This is not as difficult as you may think. Again, keep notes. By working in both directions, inwardly and outwardly, you are establishing contact with the element of Air as it exists for you and the reality of everyday life. This is real Magic.

One day, you will probably feel the need to purchase or make a real Sword. You will have the advantage of knowing what this Sword is and what it means to you. It will be a true Magic Sword, as opposed to being based on someone else's mistaken ideals about Magic. Because you first worked with inner reality using symbolism, your Magic Sword will serve as an instant contact, in a highly personal sense, with power as expressed through the element of Air. The choice is yours, for the Sword has two edges and cuts both ways. Will you choose superstition and acceptance, or reality and true power?

The Rod (or Wand) (Fire)

The Magic Rod (or Wand) (sometimes the Spear) is somewhat like the Sword, subject to much speculation. Let us start by looking at the reality that lies behind this important symbol. The Rod represents the element Fire. Rods represent rulership, control, authority and, power.

They equate to the fixed sign of Leo, the sign of regality. Note how the symbol of the Rod constantly shows itself. From the baton the conductor uses to direct the orchestra to the parliamentary mace used in England to the staff of the wise person to the crosier of a bishop.

Unlike the Sword, the Rod must be made. The more individual each weapon, the better, so there is no point in imitating the designs of others or buying a ready-made Rod. Spend some time thinking about the Rod—what it means, what it represents. As with the Sword, work with the inner reality before you decide on the final design. The Magic Rod represents a powerful positive link between Heaven and Earth, or power and activity. The purpose of Magic is the use of power to produce physical results and, this ought to be incorporated into the Rod.

Be realistic and incorporate meaningful magical practice into the process of making your Rod. It is simply no use hacking down some convenient piece of tree and then writing obscure symbols on it. Think. Use your ingenuity and imagination all through the process. Start by carefully selecting the wood—which type are you going to use? (Hazel is traditional, but the choice is yours). What length? What natural characteristics should the piece have?

Select your wood, cut it to length and, then add to it. Perhaps the tip could have some symbol of power attached to it, such as a small cross or gemstone, or better still a meteorite. Affix a symbol of Earth to the opposite end, such as a plain black stone or an Encircled Cross. Look at the length of wood representing the connecting link between these two points. You could paint it white to represent light and paint a band at the halfway point to represent the Sun. Or, you could paint alternate bands of colors to represent the planets. Starting at the top, paint black (Saturn), blue (Jupiter), red (Mars), gold The Sun), green (Venus), orange (Mercury) and, finally silver (the Moon). This looks very impressive and is symbolically correct. Power starts at the top, works its way through the planets and, impacts itself into Earth reality. When working with this Rod in planetary Magic, hold the Rod in different positions, depending on the planet being conjured.

There are many other possibilities, such as the Spear concept. Your Rod could be painted red to represent Fire. A metal tip is fitted on one end, black to represent power entering Earth existence, while the opposite end could be painted gold or perhaps have a small gemstone set in it to represent the power of light. The possibilities are endless, but you must decide, and you must make this important symbol, for it is personal involvement that produces a true Rod of power.

The Cup (Water)

The Magic Cup represents the essence of life, the overflowing of divine love. The Cup refreshes, rejuvenates, revitalizes. It is the divine mother, the grand lady of Nature. The Cup is supplication, humility. The magical operations undertaken are prayer, purification and, healing.

The Cup is not a weapon at all; it is a container. However, it is no less a potent symbol than the other three. The Sword and Rod are active, for they help us do things, either by thought or by action. The Cup and Shield are passive, for they receive. The eternal waters of life are contained in the Cup, which you drink from whenever you have need. The Shield receives your earthy plan of action or belief patterns that mold your life.

The Cup is the only container on the Magic Circle. Cups contain, but contain what? The answer is: everything. The element of Water symbolizes consciousness and, those who have spent time on magical matters will realize that consciousness is that magical something that renders the inert into the living. Without consciousness, or life energy, an object cannot exist. Everything must contain consciousness, even a seemingly dead piece of rock. The supposed dead rock is very much alive. Its atoms and molecules are in constant vibration and movement, even though we cannot see them.

The Cup contains everything; everything contains consciousness; and consciousness responds to magical intent through the mind, the imagination and, the emotions. Working together in their most powerful and purest forms, the mind, the imagination and, the emotions create love. Just as Nature bestows abundant water, without which life could not exist, so Jupiter bestows total abundance, without strings or conditions. This is love in its highest form. So often, earthly love is completely misunderstood and possessive. Real love gives freedom. Real love implies no conditions. To give a Cup is to love completely. You are symbolically giving that person the means to acquire his or her highest aspirations, without conditions, without boundaries.

Spend some considerable time working with this symbol and attuning to it by any means that ingenuity can suggest. Think about your Cup. Get to know your Cup in your own way. Look for Cups in everyday life and meditate on the symbol, gradually building up a personal familiarity. Do not copy other people's ideas. Imitation never is effective in magical working.

The idea behind the Cup matters, not the actual physical representation. Do not rush out and buy expensive gold or silver plate or be disappointed if someone gives you a Cup made of pottery or plain glass. The inner reality, the ability to work with the symbol *through* the physical object, is what really matters.

I often think that give and take are much misunderstood. While it is wrong to constantly take without giving, it is equally wrong to give and not to take. If someone offers you a gift, take it! Not only will you make them happy, you will also open channels for further giving and taking. Quite often, the inability to accept gifts is only the tip of the iceberg and, a deep subconscious problem prevents you from receiving life's benefits.

For life itself needs to give. If you do not take, you effectively block up the creative process and harm yourself. Always accept, even if you cannot use the gift. You can always give it to someone else.

Your Magic Cup is your link with life and its natural abundance, so use it as such. The Cup has many magical uses. Here is just one suggestion. Fill the Cup with good, clear water and, think and meditate on all I have said. Contemplate abundance and allow it to flow into the water. Drink the water and let this abundance flow into your life. Life holds this promise to those who seek reality through valid symbols such as this. From the lowliest of cupped hands to the Graal itself lies a path of beneficence far beyond expectations for those who seek to receive. So ask freely through the Cup and allow life to fulfill its purpose of creative, never-ending abundance.

The Shield (Earth)

The Magic Shield represents inert matter, the material world, with all its hardships and struggles. It is the darkest state of being. Its use is to represent ethereal qualities upon the material plane and is analogous to salt, which preserves flesh and thus material existence.

What exactly is a Magic Shield? What does it do and how do we use it? Very few magical books attempt to answer these very practical questions, preferring instead to perpetuate meaningless superstition.

The Magic Shield belongs to magical north and the element of Earth. Do not take the word Earth too literally—I do not mean soil or planet Earth. The true element of Earth is inert matter, that is, matter without life or form—although it is not possible on this planet for anything to be truly inert, for everything contains life energy and as such is already molded by Nature. A fair analogy would be to equate matter with a lump of clay. As it stands, it is quite useless, it has no form. However, by molding the clay, we can produce anything from a flat plate to a statue, according to our will, our creative abilities and, of course our imagination. We conceive an idea and turn it into physical reality by molding the clay to our needs. We give it form.

Suppose we are way back in time. There is lots of fresh water, but we have no means of drinking other than by using cupped hands. All we have is formless clay. First comes an idea: a vessel or container inspired by our cupped hands. This first seed idea equates to the element of Fire. Now the imagination is brought into play as the idea is shaped in the mind, until a clear picture exists. This imaginative process equates to the element of Water. The element of Air is brought into play by taking the clay and by using skill and ingenuity to shape it into a physical representation of the mental picture. The final outcome is the vessel itself and, this equates to the element of Earth. An inert, shapeless mass has now become a useful vessel. Both equate to Earth, yet they are different by virtue of the fact that an idea has changed the shape of the clay and given it form. The element of Earth is directly connected to the material side of life and, to control Earth we must shape it accordingly. We must impress on it the pattern of our true desires. This is where the Magic Shield comes into the picture.

If we wish to build a house, we draw a plan. If we want to build an electronic circuit, we produce a circuit diagram. Or if we wish to express an idea, we write it down. All of these are Shield functions, because we are bringing ideas into physical fact by producing a plan of action. In Magic, the Shield represents inert matter and the design represents the plan of action. In other words, it is a symbolic representation of that which we wish to bring into physical reality. For example, suppose our intention is to increase our earnings. First we collect the facts and, then we produce a design to represent this. The traditional planet for money is Venus, whose color is green and whose mental is copper. A Shield representation of this would therefore be a green Shield bearing the symbol of Venus in copper-colored paint. The four sevens from the tarot deck could be affixed at the cardinal points, to represent the four worlds and, the intention could be written along the edge. Here you have a perfectly sane and sensible Shield that represents an intention and a plan of action.

The only problem with this particular scheme is that you would need a new Shield for other intentions. A time-consuming and costly process. The alternatives now given are far more suitable. The first thing is to acquire a suitable Shield. Now, for heaven's sake, if you are going to make a Shield, at least let it look like a Shield. A realistic size is about eighteen inches in diameter. This can be cut from stiff card, plywood, or hardboard. Paint one side black to represent matter and the other side white to represent power. Either use the white side to project an imaginary picture onto the surface (which with practice is not as difficult as you may think) or paint on it a universal symbol that covers all possibilities. The design is entirely up to you and your requirements, but a useful suggestion is presented in figure 5 (see page 50). This particular design has the advantage of incorporating all the elements, planets and, signs of the Zodiac, therefore covering all possibilities. It requires a little skill and patience to make, but it is well worth the effort. Not only is it fully functional in a practical sense, but it is also a valuable symbol for contemplation and meditation in its own right and will reveal much to those who take the trouble to work with it.

The Shield itself is no guarantee of success. The Shield is not magical; it is only a focus for your mind. However, the more you think about it and work with it, the more magical your mind will become, for one enhances the other. All that nonsense about buying magical weapons made to the specifications given in some grimoire and then expecting power to flow into your life is just that—nonsense.

⊙ The Sun	♃ Jupiter	○ Air	
☽ The Moon	♄ Saturn	△ Fire	
☿ Mercury	♅ Uranus	☽ Water	
♀ Venus	♆ Neptune	▢ Earth	
♂ Mars	♇ Pluto		

Figure 5. The Magic Shield.

A true magical weapon is a tool. It has to be first conceived in the mind and then brought gradually into physical being using thought and skill. You not only produce an individual weapon, which will act as a focus for your mind and a control symbol for power, you also follow the example given in the Shield, namely: conceive, create, craft, and consolidate.

Meditation, the Cosmic Sphere, and the Inner Temple

In all forms of real Magic, it is the inner work (for example, meditative work performed in the imagination) that gets results. Magic without this inner work is pointless.

Magical Meditation

Meditation enables you to penetrate inner secrets that are obscured by conscious thought. Magical meditation is a tool and bears little resemblance to the strange, pseudo-Eastern methods that have become the norm. In magical meditation, focus the mind on an idea or symbol and allow the mind to bring up useful facts or realizations. To aid concentration, bring together words, colors, scents, sounds, and so forth, which correspond to the aspect under investigation. This is the true purpose of ritual.

Let us continue our discussion of meditation with the Magic Sword. First, throw out any ideas that the Sword is used to command demons or spirits and so forth. This is purely superstition. The Sword is the control symbol for the element of Air and can be used in two ways:

1. As a meditation symbol.
2. As a means of directing those energies that equate to the element of Air.

The Sword represents all that is Air. However, much depends on your ability to understand and contact this element. In a nutshell, if you do not know much about the element, then the Sword will be of little use. The process of building up control over this element is then twofold: first, learn about the element, and second, learn about the control symbol.

Learning about the element (or any type of energy) requires that you use observation and meditation. In the first instance you will need to look around at everyday objects and situations while looking for Sword-like similarities. This takes a little practice, but is well worth the trouble. Keep a magical notebook in which to record any observations and lists of acquired attributions. This need not be done at specific times or as a ritual; instead it should become a habit of looking at life along a specific channel, in this case through the element of Air.

Observation looks at the physical side of life, through a narrow slit, to help the mind focus and thereby understand a specific mode of power. With meditation, you use a narrowing down of perspective, this time by using a symbol in order to get the subconscious mind to throw out meaningful images and ideas. In the case of Air, you use the symbol of the Sword. To do this, erect the Cosmic Sphere, as described (see figure 4, page 37). Then focus the attention on magical east. Imagine a yellow doorway with the symbol of Air on it. Pass through the door and see a Sword suspended in the air. From now on, let your imagination work for you. Do not visualize, but rather allow images and ideas to arise quite naturally. This takes a little practice and may at first be disappointing in terms of actual information. However, persevere and you will learn much in the way of real information as to the nature of this element and the purpose of the weapon.

Do not expect instant enlightenment and a wealth of powerful magical secrets to pour forth. This is not the way it usually works. Quite often, the student must start with little, working slowly and patiently toward the acquisition of knowledge and power.

Record any impressions in your notebook. Use brief notes only; there is no need for long-winded essays. All you need is something that will stimulate the memory at some future date. Also, it is often difficult in the initial stages to understand your impressions and the images they evoke. This is due to the fact that you are dealing with the subconscious mind, which, as you know, does not speak English (or any other language). You will, however, find these notes very valuable someday. Regular meditation along a specific channel such as this does far more than provide useful notes—it helps you to attune to that energy in a way that is not immediately apparent. Put another way, it helps you get the feel of that energy by familiarity.

The subconscious mind works in two ways. First, it feeds back information likely to be of use, and second, it provides power that can be directed according to will. Naturally, the more you understand the type of energy being worked, the better the result.

Also, knowing how this energy manifests in terms of rulership is bound to increase success.

It is always the rule that those who know are bound to be more adept or successful than those who only *think* that they know. Imagine that you buy a Magic Sword, stand in an Encircled Cross symbol that you just painted on the floor, and simply expect the gods to bestow numerous blessings at your command. Ridiculous! Now consider that you take time to properly erect an Encircled Cross, develop it into a Cosmic Sphere (a process you will learn in this chapter), direct your full attention toward magical east, and use the control symbol of Air (the Sword) to conjure energy (direct it) toward your intended goal. Which technique is more likely to produce results?

Erection of the Cosmic Sphere

The Cosmic Sphere is a vital step in your magical work. Practice this exercise often, preferably once a day, until you are proficient.

You will need:

•   Five candles: One white to represent the center, one each of yellow, red, blue, and green to represent the elements. Place the white candle on the altar. Place the other candles on the altar or adjacent to the appropriate temple wall using candleholders.

•   An incense burner. Place it in the south (Fire).

Begin by relaxing and clearing the mind of everyday thoughts. Light the central candle, which symbolizes your own center of power; pause and contemplate this for a while. Imagine the Universal Triangle in front of the central candle and again briefly contemplate the relationship between your subconscious mind, Universal Energy, and Divinity.

Imagine a shaft of light, rising upward, forming the path between center and Crown. Similarly, pause and try to feel that power is spiraling downward into the temple. Now imagine a shaft of light traveling down, eventually terminating at the Cube. Pause and imagine that power is now spiraling upward into the temple. The next stage is to establish the cardinal points. Imagine a shaft of light proceeding toward the east; light the yellow candle, and then imagine that a Sword appears behind it. Do the same with the other three points in turn, using the image of Magic Rod at south, Cup at west, and finally Shield at north. If you are uncertain as to the shape, size, and design of these weapons, spend some time prior to this exercise thinking about the symbols. Make drawings, contemplate the items, and try to build up an imaginary picture in your mind.

You have now established the six nodal points. All that remains is to connect these together by using the triple rings of cosmos. Start at the apex (Crown) and imagine a circle of light traveling through south, base, north, and back to top. This is Ring 1. Ring 2 (the Magic Circle) begins at east and travels clockwise through south, west, north, and back to east.

Finally, Ring 3 starts at top and travels through east, base, west, and back to top. The Cosmic Sphere is now complete.

Burn some general incense and spend some time contemplating these nodal points and their connecting paths. Consider these carefully, fix them in your mind, and allow ideas to arise uninterrupted. Gradually become more relaxed, and then concentrate on one aspect only. This can be a point or a path; the choice is up to you. Hold the symbol in your mind, for example, the Sword, and then let the imagination take over to see what happens. Perhaps you may find yourself walking toward the Sword, picking it up, and looking along the blade toward the point. Do not strain; allow imagery to work in its own way. Magical meditation, such as this, will reveal much. At first, the images and ideas may not make any immediate sense. Do not spend too much time trying to rationalize them; instead, make brief notes for future reference. Let me assure you that eventually they will prove to be very valuable indeed.

Meditating on a path is also quite simple. Take hold of one of the symbols (magical weapons) and imagine that you are walking along a path toward the center. This is only one possibility—what is more important is that you become involved with the Cosmic Sphere in your own way by using your own ideas and letting your imagination work fully.

At conclusion, close down by reversing the procedure. Start at north, extinguish the candle, and imagine the shafts of light disappearing into the center. Continue this through west, south, and east. Finally, see the vertical shafts return to center, extinguish the central candle, and leave the temple to write down any observations.

The Cosmic Sphere
Becomes the Inner Temple

Erect the Cosmic Sphere as described. The three rings of the Cosmic Sphere form the framework for the Inner Temple. No two people will have the same ideas or visual images of an Inner Temple. Each one is different by virtue of the fact that no two people are the same. It is therefore not possible for me to give you an exact guide as to what shape or form it will take. I can, however, help you find your own way by using this specially constructed exercise. This exercise will help you contact your subconscious mind in a special way, which will then cause the subconscious to give you ideas and images from which you can build this vital state of inner awareness.

Find somewhere quiet, preferably a spare room, or if you are lucky enough, a temple. Relax and clear the mind of everyday thoughts, then perform the following exercise. Do not try to visualize or strain in any way. Simply think of the inner journey while letting your imagination work for you.

Breathe slowly and gently and relax, leaving behind all thoughts of everyday life. Let nothing concern you other than the exciting possibilities that lie ahead as you journey to a special place in the deepest recesses of your mind. It belongs to you and no one else. None can enter this place, except those few you choose to invite for reasons of your own. In this place, you are in control, you are the master, you direct, and you receive. Inside this place, there are natural forces in abundant supply. They are yours to use, yours to understand, for they are part of you—they are life force and they give form under your direction. Relax and let the vast potential of your subconscious mind work for you, for this is the secret of all magical work.

Imagine before you a door that leads to your Inner Temple. It is not difficult to enter because this is your doorway to your own inner reality.

No one can prevent access to this inner realm, and there is nothing to fear, for nothing harmful can ever exist here. In your imagination, walk toward the door, reach out your hand, and touch the door. It opens quite easily. Pass through the door and find yourself in a large square room.

Emblazoned on the floor is the symbol of the Encircled Cross. It seems to be made of pure light, and its color changes constantly in what appears to be a random pattern. Yet the pattern is not random, for the colors change in conformance with the tides of Nature. Move to the center and look around. Set in the middle of each of the four walls is a doorway, and you can pass through any one of these as you will. A small circular pool of water rests in the center of this Inner Temple.

Now direct your attention above, see the symbol of the Crown and let your mind consider that which is God. Power flows from this point as you will. See this as bright light pouring downward in abundance.

Now direct your attention toward magical east. Immediately in front of you there is a yellow door with a Sword set above it. On this door you see the tarot card 10 of Swords. Touch it and it opens, revealing a path that leads toward the rising Sun at dawn. You feel a gentle breeze blowing softly against your skin. Now allow the light that came from above to enter your Inner Temple. This light is yellow.

Direct your attention toward magical south. To your right, there is a red door with a Magic Rod set above it. On this door is the tarot card 10 of Wands. Touch this door and it opens, revealing a path that is lit by the midday Sun. Feel the warmth of the summer day. Allow red light to enter the Inner Temple.

Now direct your attention toward magical west. Behind you is a blue door with a Cup set above it, and on this door is the tarot card 10 of Cups. Touch this door and it opens, revealing a path that gently leads down to the sea, lit by the setting Sun. feel the cool of the evening and allow the blue light to enter through the western door.

Finally, to your left, the north, is a green door with a Magic Shield set above it. On this door is the tarot card 10 of Pentacles. Touch this door and it opens, revealing a path lit only by starlight. Feel the peace and tranquility of the night and allow bright green light to enter through this door.

All four doors are now open. Go back to the pool in the center of this temple and mediate on this power and its purpose. Look into its depths. The pool will give you answers to your questions. Allow images to come into your mind.[1] The duration of the pool meditation can be entirely up to you, although five minutes usually suffices. After sufficient time has passed, see each elemental colored light pass out through each of the elemental doorways, realizing that it will now work its way into physical existence, epitomized by the lowermost point of the Cosmic Sphere, the Cubic Black Stone. Before you is another door with an Encircled Cross carved deeply into the wood. Touch this door, see it open, pass through it, and you are back in your own world once more. Close down the Cosmic Sphere and make notes.

Others have searched and found their own place. Now you must do the same. This task is not difficult; in fact, it is far easier than you think. All you have to do is desire and you will find this place. I cannot describe it for you, for you are the only person who knows where it is and what it looks like. It may be a cave, a secret grove, a temple set on top of a mountain or deep beneath the earth. Seek and you will find it. You may return as often as you wish, for this place belongs to you. It has many secrets and contains much in the way of practical knowledge in magical matters.

---

[1] You may substitute a crystal or Magic mirror, but do not forget that these are substitutes.

So often the images from the depths of our subconscious mind appear to be difficult to translate because we are learning a new language, that of symbolism. But if you persevere, you will eventually learn the ways of the inner mind. When you are familiar with this inner journey and have found that special place, your own Inner Temple, you may ritualize this by erecting the triple rings of cosmos, as described, and then use your imagination to enter the now familiar Inner Temple. By performing your magical work within this framework you will notice a distinct improvement, because you are dealing directly with your subconscious mind in a highly personal way. If you have the will and the patience to find it, the Inner Temple will teach you many things in a way that is difficult to describe. Once you find it, keep it to yourself; keep it a secret, for this place is not meant to be the subject of general discussion.

Seeing Two Things at Once in Your Mind's Eye

How is it possible to see the Cosmic Sphere in the mind's eye while imagining something else, such as opening the Cosmic Sphere and imagining the four doorways inside the Inner Temple?

It is all a question of memory. To imagine several different things all at the same time is difficult if not impossible. Fortunately, you do not need to do this. As you build up the Cosmic Sphere, you establish each part in your memory. You move on through each successive stage, concentrating only on whatever is necessary. For example, you imagine the central light, then you imagine the first of the six arms. There is no need to keep the image of the central light constantly in your imagination because it exists in your memory. You use this and similar procedures in everyday life. For instance, suppose you were standing in a room facing a window. You would see the window quite clearly. Now if you turned around to face the opposite wall, you would see the wall; however, you would still know that the window existed, because you had just seen it. You could recall it in your imagination because its image is stored in your memory. In a similar fashion, having become familiar with the room, you would know what the room looked like in totality without actually seeing it physically.

It is exactly the same with the Cosmic Sphere—using your imagination to build up an imaginary room in your memory. All through the building up procedure you establish each stage before moving on to the next. Therefore, you are free to concentrate on the pool because you know the Cosmic Sphere exists in your memory.

Because this Cosmic Sphere is imaginary it would be easy to dismiss the entire concept as being worthless, but this is not the case. Any deliberate erection of a symbolic pattern will affect the subconscious mind, because you are using what is, in effect, a powerful language that the subconscious mind understands. It is therefore necessary to treat these symbols with respect and practice using them often. It should also be borne in mind that symbols are not holy or sacred, so to worship them is sheer folly. Likewise, they are not meant to be worn as ornaments or lucky charms; people who do so show a marked lack of understanding as to the real nature of symbols.

Magical Rituals

A magical ritual is simply a way to focus the mind, the emotions, and the imagination on a specific intention, be it purely practical or esoteric. Rituals therefore help us to concentrate along a specified channel of awareness. A fair comparison would be to the use of a radio receiver. You use the tuning knob to select a station with great accuracy, and then you enhance this signal by adjusting the tone and volume controls. A magical ritual works the same way by helping the magician to home in on selected patterns of energy.

There are several general phases to a ritual. First, and most important, is to clarify your intention. There is a very good reason for this. A half-hearted intention simply does not get down to subconscious levels, because the normal conscious barriers are still there. Prior to the ritual, think through your intentions carefully and note any doubts and uncertainties when they come streaming up from subconscious levels into your conscious mind. You must bypass these things, so think around them positively until you get your intention absolutely and utterly clear in your mind. When you perform the ritual, your mind will not be swamped by negative thoughts, doubts, and uncertainties. Your mind must be crystal clear; otherwise you stand very little chance of succeeding.

Regarding intentions, it is really important to start small and gradually build slowly and certainly on each success. Until you practice Magic, you cannot truly believe. And until you truly believe, you cannot use Magic. So by starting with small magical operations it is easier to trick yourself over the threshold of doubt. That way you stand a far better chance of success.

Next, plan the ritual. That means attending to all the bits and pieces that will be used, such as candles, incense, color of altar cloths, and so forth. Once the details are sorted out, everything should be very clear in your mind and you should be very confident about what you are doing.

Next, enter the temple and relax. Clear your mind, and when you are fully relaxed, start to bring the mind to the intention. Now you are ready to open the temple using the cosmic rings, perform the ritual, and then close down the ritual in the customary fashion.

Life's Energies

As we are dealing with esoteric matters, the bulk of your work will be concerned with investigating life's energies and discovering inner truths. There has to be a system of classifying energies so that they may be identified more easily. The ideal system of classification is the Cabalistic Tree of Life, of which more will be said later. In the meantime, we will consider a simpler scheme based on the planets.

Planetary Rituals

Following is the general procedure for Planetary Magic.

Attending to the Outer Work.

In order to aid concentration and help create the correct atmosphere or mood, it is necessary to bring into the temple physical objects that help suggest the planet being worked with. In the case of Mercury, for example, this could be done by using the correct planetary color. An altar cloth of plain white with the planetary glyph painted in orange is useful, also orange, mercurial incense and perhaps an altar symbol of the Caduceus. There are no hard and fast rules to follow, for it is all a question of individual choice and personal involvement with the rite. There is no substitute for careful planning, individual effort, and ingenuity. Half-hearted attempts and blind acceptance of the written word are bound to produce poor results, so plan carefully and get involved, even if it does take the edge off your enthusiasm for a while. The effective rituals are those you devise for yourself. The esoteric tyro wants prepackaged rituals and is perpetually anxious about "doing it right." If that is still your problem, then you have not been paying attention.

Attending to the Inner Work.

Rituals that do not contain the inner work in the imagination are really quite pointless. It makes no difference how much equipment you use or, in the case of ready-made scripts, how well you speak or intone the words. Unless the imagination is used and is on target, the whole affair will be a waste of time and effort. The general procedure ought to be:

1. Open the temple by using the cosmic rings, thereby establishing the Cosmic Sphere.
2. Use the imagination to see and enter the Inner Cubic Temple.
3. Focus the mind on the appropriate planet by using the faces of the Cube.
4. On completion of work, close down by using the imagination to leave the Cube and then close down the Cosmic Sphere.

Before working with the planets in detail, it is always a good idea to practice this procedure and become familiar with the inner cubic structure. This can be the basis of a meditation in which you explore the Cube by turning your attention toward each face for a few minutes. Let impressions rise up in the mind and, of course, keep brief notes of these excursions. When you are familiar with the Cube, you may then proceed with the more specific work connected with each individual planet.

Magic Words and Words of Power

Before moving on to a complete planetary ritual, we ought to look at speech and those so-called words of power. Don't presume that the speaking of certain ancient words or divine names will, all by itself, cause power to flow or cause miracles to happen. No matter what the books say, this is nonsense! No word or statement contains power—power lies within the mind of the person who speaks those words. Just like equipment, words are tools and are used for the sole purpose of aiding concentration. Let me give you an example:

Say to yourself, either out loud or in your mind, "I feel good." Now say this several times with *feeling*. In other words, *mean* what you are saying.

I feel good. (Repeat this several times.)

Can you see the difference? You use your emotions to put power into these words. Finally, repeat the words several times and use your imagination to see yourself pulsating with energy and goodness. Do this with conviction for a minute or so. There is a considerable difference between the original approach and the final one. The words have not changed, but the inner work has given power to these words. This is the real secret of words of power. The difference in magical work is astonishing.

This is an important thing with rituals. If words are going to be used, they should be meant. Words of power work because the person puts feeling, belief, and imagination into those words. Nonmagic words—the vocabulary of the human race—hinder real communication. They are used to conceal facts, propagate illusion, and replace reality. Humans are born thinking in pictures and sensations. We are then conditioned to think in words. Magic words emanate from the heart. Dead words and illusion are born of the intellect.

For instance, a person faces a particular quarter and says, "I declare this quarter open." It is one thing to say those words and not think about them, but it is another to vividly see that doorway opening up, that color pouring into the temple, with feeling and imagination.

Master Ritual

Here is a Master Ritual that can be used for all planetary work. It needs a good deal of practice to make it work. You do not need to use all of the suggestions or even the words, because your individual choice is more important. Change or modify whatever you wish, but do remember that the basic format should be followed:

1. Open the temple by using the Cosmic Sphere of three rings.
2. Enter the Inner Temple, which, in the initial stages, consists of the Cube.
3. Perform the main magical work.
4. Close down the temple.

Before starting, the intention should be clear in the mind and all equipment should be in place. Spend some time relaxing and clearing the mind of unwanted thoughts, and then gradually bring your attention to bear on the work to be performed. To aid concentration, it is better if the temple or workroom is in darkness, with only a small candle burning along with some neutral incense or joss sticks. This helps to create the right atmosphere for magical work and is far better than using ordinary electric lighting. When ready, stand up and say:

Blessed be the inner light, mediating all that is and will ever be.

Light the central candle.

Use your imagination to see a bright light building up within your heart. See a shaft of light rise vertically upward from your heart and say:

Blessed be the Crown of creation.

Imagine the Crown.

Now see a shaft of light proceeding downward from your heart and say:

Blessed be the throne of Earth.

Imagine the Cube of Earth at base.

Now imagine a shaft of light proceeding toward magical east.

See the symbol of the Sword and say:

Blessed be the portal of Air.

Light the eastern candle.

Imagine a shaft of light proceeding from your heart toward magical south and say:

Blessed be the portal of Fire.

Light the southern candle.

Imagine a shaft of light proceeding from your heart to magical west and say:

Blessed be the portal of Water.

Light the western candle.

Finally, see a shaft of light proceeding from your heart to magical north and say:

Blessed be the portal of Earth.

Light the northern candle.
Now say:

I now declare this temple duly open.

The next stage is one of entering the Inner Temple. Imagine a doorway in front of you and say:

Let the doorway to the Inner Temple be opened.

See the door open and imagine that you step through this into the Inner Temple. Say:

Before me—Mercury. (see the orange wall)

To my right—Mars. (see the red wall)

Behind me—Jupiter. (see the blue wall)

To my left—Venus. (see the green well)

Above me—Saturn. (see the black ceiling)

Below me—the Moon. (see the silver floor)

In the center, the altar of the Sun. This should be imagined as a cube of solid gold that appears to radiate golden light.

Light planetary candles and incense followed by the main body of the work. In the initial stages, this may be simply an exercise in exploring this Inner Temple in the imagination. Later on, you will of course concentrate on one planet. You may find it helpful to focus your attention toward the appropriate wall (or floor/ceiling), looking for symbols, or simply letting ideas arise from the subconscious mind. There are no hard and fast rules, just follow your instincts and let your imagination lead you rather than trying to be logical.

At conclusion, extinguish the planetary candles and say:

Let there be peace within this place.

See the door, pass through it once more, and let it close behind you. Extinguish the eastern candle and say:

Let there be peace to the east.

See the Sword disappear. Now extinguish the southern candle and say:

Let there be pace to the south.

See the Rod disappear. Extinguish the western candle and say:

Let there be peace to the west.

See the Cup disappear. Extinguish the northern candle and say:

Let there be peace to the north.

See the Shield disappear. Now say:

Let there be peace above.

See the Crown disappear.

And let there be peace below.

See the Cube disappear. Finally, make the closing statement:

I *now declare this temple duly closed.*

Extinguish central candle and leave the temple to consider ideas that have arisen and write up any notes for future reference.

Planetary Correspondences

THE SUN

Glyph: ⊙
Color: Gold or yellow
Metal: Gold or gold-colored
Incense: Frankincense
Altar symbol: Hexagram
Magical direction on Cube: Center
Tarot cards: Air-6 of Swords; Fire-6 of Wands; Water-6 of Cups; Earth-6 of Pentacles

THE MOON

Glyph: ☽

Color: Silver

Metal: Silver or silver-colored

Incense: Jasmine

Altar symbol: Crescent Moon

Magical direction on Cube: Below

Tarot cards: Air-9 of Swords; Fire-9 of Wands; Water-9 of Cups; Earth-9 of Pentacles

MERCURY

Glyph: ☿

Color: Orange

Metal: Brass

Incense: Lavender or Storax (often commercially sold as Styrax)

Altar symbol: Caduceus

Magical direction on Cube: East

Tarot cards: Air-8 of Swords; Fire-8 of Wands; Water-8 of Cups; Earth-8 of Pentacles

VENUS

Glyph: ♀

Color: Green

Metal: Copper

Incense: Rose

Altar symbol: A Rose or a Dove

Magical direction on Cube: North

Tarot cards: Air-7 of Swords; Fire-7 of Wands; Water-7 of Cups; Earth-7 of Pentacles

MARS

Glyph: ♂
Color: Red
Metal: Iron
Incense: Benzoin
Altar symbol: Pentagram
Magical direction on Cube: South
Tarot cards: Air-5 of Swords; Fire-5 of Wands; Water-5 of Cups; Earth-5 of Pentacles

JUPITER

Glyph: ♃
Color: Blue
Metal: Tin
Incense: Sandalwood
Altar symbol: An Equal-Armed Cross or a Blue Square
Magical direction on Cube: West
Tarot cards: Air-4 of Swords; Fire-4 of Wands; Water-4 of Cups; Earth-4 of Pentacles

SATURN

Glyph: ♄
Color: Black
Metal: Lead
Incense: Musk
Altar symbol: A Black Triangle

Magical direction on Cube: Above

Tarot cards: Air-3 of Swords; Fire-3 of Wands; Water-3 of Cups; Earth-3 of Pentacles

NEPTUNE

Glyph: ♆

Color: Gray

Metal: None; coral or anything from the sea is useful

Incense: Ambergris

Altar symbol: Trident

Magical direction on Cube: West or is the Cube itself

Tarot cards: Air-2 of Swords; Fire-2 of Wands; Water-2 of Cups; Earth-2 of Pentacles

URANUS

Glyph: ♅

Color: White or transparent

Metal: Platinum, uranium (aluminum or zinc may be used)

Incense: Civet

Altar symbol: The Spinning Cross or a White Chaos Star

Magical direction on Cube: East or the idea of the Cube

Tarot cards: Air-Ace of Swords; Fire-Ace of Wands; Water-Ace of Cups; Earth-Ace of Pentacles

PLUTO

Glyph: ♇ or ⯓

Color: Violet or luminous blue

Metal: Tungsten (iron may be used)

Incense: Peat Moss or Opopanax

Altar symbol: Phoenix
Magical direction on Cube: West or the center
Tarot cards: None

The Cabalistic Tree of Life

Sooner or later, every serious student of Esoteric Magic will encounter the mysteries of the Cabalistic Tree of Life. This system is by far the best symbolic basis for growth available today. The problems existing within the system stem not so much from its structure as from the way in which it has been altered to suit personal fetishes. Let us now look at the Tree of Life from first principles in an effort to establish the reality of the system and show its undoubted value in contemporary Magic.

The Tree of Life is a plan of potential—your potential. It is not a holy symbol to be placed on a wall or altar and prayed to, nor is it a symbolic ladder by which we evolve. It is simply a plan of energy flow, rather like a circuit diagram or a Cosmic Sphere plan that helps us locate where we are at any given point in time.

There are two ways in which to view this symbol. First, it is our own plan for success (whatever success means to each individual), and second, it is a plan of the cosmic scheme as a whole. There are two distinct ways of using the Tree of Life: practically to solve life's problems, or esoterically, for those who wish to study the greater scheme of things. The Tree of Life is highly individual, and each person must relate to the symbol in his or her own way. Naturally, there is a basic framework based on cosmic law and truth, but then it is up to you to discover the potential of the system by using your own attributions, which flow freely from your own subconscious mind. Let us now look at this basic framework.

If you are attempting to understand the workings of the cosmos, how would you do this? Well, the simplest way is to split this up into manageable units that can then be examined in detail. Perhaps the best way of looking at this is to equate the entire cosmic scheme to pure white light.

The color white is the sum total of all other colors. Only when you use a prism do you see these colors. It is exactly the same with the Tree of Life; it helps us understand the whole by looking at the lesser parts. Everything that has, is, or will ever be, can be found within the pattern of the Tree. Such is its power.

The First Lesson

Look at the diagram of the Tree of Life given in figure 6 on page 79. The Tree of Life consists of ten spheres plus Daath, twenty-two traditional paths, and three columns of pillars. What else can you see? In learning the secrets of the Tree, the first lesson is one of observation.

When you started to study this book, you were confronted with a symbol: the Encircled Cross. As a simple diagram, it could quite easily have been left without as much as a second glance; however, as you now know, it can be expanded into a Cosmic Sphere and an Inner Temple. In short, when someone takes the time and trouble to look behind the obvious, many mysteries and real magical secrets are duly revealed. Symbols are not to be prayed to, hung around your neck, or propped up on an altar—they are tools. The first lesson is always one of looking at the symbol to see what comes to mind rather than accepting the commonly held view that such things are sacred or holy or must be revered in some way.

When using a symbol as a means of discovery, remember two points:

1.   All symbols conform to universal laws and therefore exhibit these laws.

2.   To be fully effective, all preconceived ideas should be pushed aside, thereby allowing the symbol to communicate in an individualistic way.

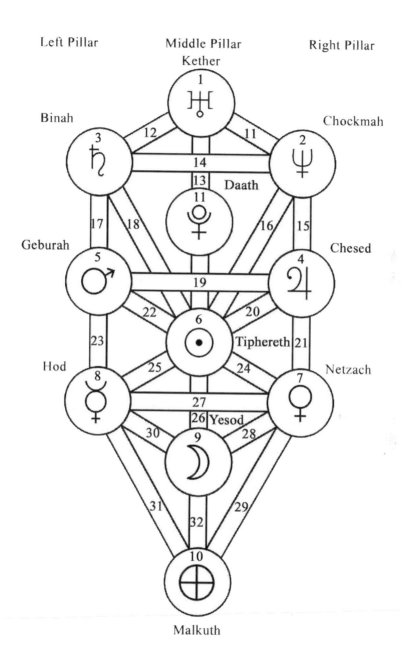

Figure 6. The Tree of Life.

Looking at the Encircled Cross once more, you can see that it clearly exhibits certain laws, as in point one, page 78. Notice how the circle encompasses all. Everything exists within the circle. Notice how the circle indicates the never-ending cycle of cosmic activity as seen in the seasons of the year or the revolution of the Earth around the Sun. Within the circle is the cross of the elements with its central point of power. All matter responds to the elemental forces and contains the fourfold division. Everything in creation conforms to the symbol of the Encircled Cross and the symbol itself displays the way in which creation works. Naturally, all magicians who wish to be truly creative and/or desire to know about creation use this symbol as a point of concentration, contemplation, or meditation, for, as a basis for magical work—it cannot be bettered.

In learning the secrets of real Magic, point two is the key. By allowing the symbol to speak, free from superstition and unrealistic attributions, the truth, as it applies to you, is bound to manifest.

First Principles

With these facts in mind, look again at the Tree of Life diagram. The entire Tree of Life represents all, that is, everything in existence on every level. It is a complete plan of life and of life's energies. Nothing can therefore exist outside the Tree-plan, or, put bluntly, if it does not fit on the Tree, it cannot exist.

This rule is unalterable, but it does provide two valuable ways of using the symbol:

1. We can fit any object, situation, or eventuality onto the Tree, thereby understanding it better.

2. We can use the Tree to explain the causes behind these things.

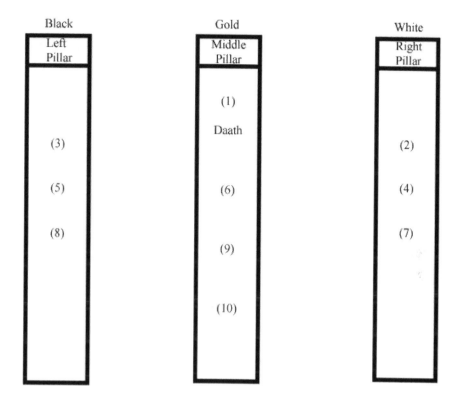

Figure 7. The Three Pillars.

The Three Pillars

Before taking a detailed look at the spheres and paths, we ought to look at the entire scheme in a general sense. The spheres are arranged in three columns, or pillars (see figure 7).

Why three? Why not two or four? One thing that you will learn about the Tree of Life is that not only will it answer questions, it also poses questions, and by thinking and searching with your mind you get not only more meaningful answers but also firsthand knowledge about the real Tree of Life.

What does the number three conjure up in your imagination? Three is the number of stability. A table with only two legs will fall over. Add one more leg, making three, and it becomes stable. After this you can add as many legs as you like and it will not make much difference—three represents stability. So we can conclude that the entire Tree of Life rests on a perfectly stable configuration of three pillars.

We live in a three-dimensional world of height, length, and width. Do you know which of these belongs to the appropriate pillar? Think about this; in fact, take every idea that contains the number three and see how it fits on the pillars. This is the right way to use the Tree by personal involvement.

The pillars are three distinct ways in which the magician may find reality and use power. The right-hand pillar is positive and male-oriented; the left-hand pillar is negative, or receptive, and female; while the middle pillar is neutral. They should be considered as a general background to the Tree rather than being taken too literally.

The Right-Hand Pillar

This represents male potency and is therefore positive. Although this pillar is surmounted by the father principle (sphere 2), it is also the path of the Orphic (use of the emotions). This apparent paradox shows how the Tree of Life not only explains life but also poses questions. The answers to these questions are found within the Tree by thinking about these things. There is always an answer to these mysteries, and the exercise of solving riddles such as these will teach you more about the Tree than any long-winded explanation. Seek and you will find.

The Left-Hand Pillar

Here you meet the female receptivity and all that is classified as negative. The word "negative" does not imply negative traits such as evil or so-called Black Magic. Although these things exist, they have no place in the greater scheme of things. The Tree of Life points only to freedom and truth. Although this is the female pillar, it is also the path of Hermetic students (those who use the mind). There is an apparent contradiction in which the female principle appears to be related to a male mode of action (using the power of thought). This is yet another riddle to be solved. A clue to the solution will be discovered by looking at the lower sphere (sphere 8) and by thinking about polarity (Female path—Male mode of expression). Give this some thought; in other words, become a true Cabalist—one who seeks to know the Tree of Life by discovering answers to these important questions.

The Middle Pillar

The center pillar, by its very nature, suggests balance. It is also neutral. Often described as the path of the mystic, this path equates to the use of the imagination. The mystic lives in a calm, tranquil world, using the imagination to probe the secrets of life, the universe, and everything. In Magic, you use the same principle, for the imagination is the key to all power. All great works are performed by controlling and directing the mind and the emotions, then using the imagination. This is the principle of the magical trident and the secret of the pillars.

Further Considerations

1. All three pillars rest in the tenth sphere of Malkuth. All three paths originate in sphere 1, Kether, and find fruition in sphere 10, Malkuth. The obvious lesson is that there are only three ways in which power may find its way into Earth-existence (sphere 10, Malkuth). While it is possible to be biased toward one path, according to your needs or psychological makeup, all three paths are used. This is aptly seen in the Zodiac scheme of the

Triplicities: cardinal, fixed, and mutable. It can also be seen in the Christian religion as Father, Son, and Holy Spirit; in Witchcraft as The Crone, Silver Lady, and Moon Maiden, or in Magic as All-Father, Earth-Mother, and Child of Light.

2. There are many important geometric configurations to be found by relating the sphere into patterns other than the main scheme. For instance: The male path of power flows not only down the right-hand pillar but also along the path formed by sphere 2, Chockmah; 5, Geburah; and 8, Hod. Likewise, the female power follows the path of sphere 3, Binah; 4, Chesed; and 7, Netzach.

3. The Tree of Life must always be flexible. Remember that the diagram is a flat representation of a three-dimensional reality. It is a common mistake for students (and teachers) to forget this important point. Call to mind the Cosmic Sphere. It consists of three rings. These rings equate to the three pillars on the Tree of Life. Do you know which ones? The answer to the riddle lies not in the flat diagram of the Tree but in the three-dimensional reality of the Cosmic Sphere.

In order to discover the secret, we must briefly enter the realms of astrology. The Zodiac teaches us that there are three qualities: cardinal, fixed, and mutable. Cardinal equates to male, for it is assertive and initiatory in its action. Fixed signs are steady, unchangeable, and therefore neutral. Mutable signs are chargeable, adaptable, and therefore female. By relating these qualities to the rings in the Cosmic Sphere, we can discover how the rings correspond to the pillars on the Tree of Life (see figure 8, page 85).

Ring 1: Connects top, south, base, and north. It equates to the cardinal signs and therefore belongs to the right-hand pillar.

Ring 2: Connects east, south, west, and north. It equates to the fixed signs and therefore belongs to the middle pillar.

Ring 3: Connects top, east, base, and west. It equates to the mutable signs and therefore belongs to the left-hand pillar.

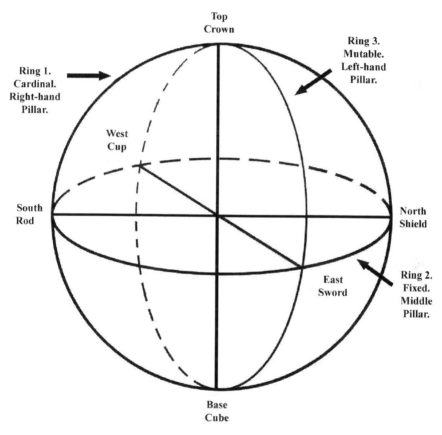

Figure 8. The Rings of the Cosmic Sphere.

The Three-Dimensional Tree of Life

Once you establish the pillars, relate the remainder of the Tree to the Cosmic Sphere. Before doing this, it is necessary to familiarize yourself with the spheres of the Tree of Life. A table of these can be found on page 87 and 88. It is by no means comprehensive, for there are many possible attributions and associations. However, as with all magical matters, it is far better to start with a few simple facts and then add to the basic scheme in the light of knowledge and common sense. A little well-understood information is always far better than endless reams of non-related information. Time is saved and confusion is avoided by adopting this approach.

In dealing with the spheres it is best to continue with the idea of simplicity first, followed by thinking carefully and questioning. The basic guidelines are easy to follow. Each sphere is a specific type of existence that is governed by a specific energy pattern. Perhaps a good example would be a village in which there are eleven houses. Each house contains a family and its belongings and has its own system of house rules. No two houses or families are the same, yet together they make up the village as a whole. If you consider the village to be the entire Tree of Life and each household a separate sphere, you will soon begin to understand how the Tree of Life works. Each sphere has four worlds, or levels. These are:

The Divine level.

The Archangelic level.

The Angelic level.

The Physical level.

This arrangement does not really tell us much; in fact, it inevitably gives the wrong impression by causing people to think that they have to bow to some god or try to evoke an angel to get anywhere. There are no gods or angels, but there are images that can, if you are well-versed in these techniques, be quite useful.

By far the best way of using each sphere is by first examining the physical end and realizing that there are three more states of existence behind it. The four worlds equate to the four elements (Air, Fire, Water, and Earth). From a practical point of view, Fire equates to ideas and power, Water equates to thinking about those ideas, Air equates to using that energy, and Earth equates to the physical end result.

Twenty-two traditional paths connect the spheres. The paths are not simply decoration or some sort of scaffolding to prop up the spheres; they are distributed in a special way and are very potent channels of energy flow. The Tree could not function without these paths (in the same way that electrical components would not work without connecting wires or printed circuits). Students of the Cabala usually make one of two classical mistakes: either they avoid the paths (preferring some fantasy world within the sphere), or they nail themselves to the cross of pathworking (which is another word for self-deluding drudgery). If you wish to use the paths correctly, first you must learn about the spheres as they really are, and then you must learn about the paths as they apply to you. Study the diagram of the Tree of Life, think about it, get to know it.

The Spheres of the Tree of Life

Sphere	Name	Color	Ruling Planet
1.	Kether	Transparent	Uranus
2.	Chockmah	White	Neptune
3.	Binah	Black	Saturn

	Daath	Ultraviolet	Pluto
4.	Chesed	Blue	Jupiter
5.	Geburah	Red	Mars
6.	Tiphereth	Gold	Sun
7.	Netzach	Green	Venus
8.	Hod	Orange	Mercury
9.	Yesod	Silver	Moon
10.	Malkuth	The Colors of the Elements	Earth

The Negative Veils

There are two ways in which we may view the Tree of Life—in its own right as a pure abstract symbol, or as a practical living structure that will enhance our lives. This chapter is concerned with the latter, although of necessity we must examine the structure in order to understand it and thereby make use of it. Traditionally there are ten spheres, together with that mysterious nonsphere, Daath. The Negative Veils are above the Tree, and some explanation of these is necessary before moving on to the main structure. I have mentioned abstraction, and in reality the only way to view the Negative Veils is by using abstractions. It is best to view these veils as yet another sphere, a sphere of nothingness. Nothing exists in exactly the same way as something; without nothing we could not have something. It is the spaces between the letters in a word or the silence between notes of music. It is the back ground against which all of mani-festation is viewed. In the science of numbers, zero is just as important as any other number. One with a zero added become ten. In our cycle of breathing there is a point at which we are not breathing; it lies between the in-breath and the out-breath. Nothing exists in its own right, and the meditation of nothing is most rewarding for those who pursue this line of light.

We have to be careful in defining nothing, and not confuse it with the absence of something. For instance, if we start with a plateful of food and eat it all, we say that there is nothing left, but this is not strictly true. The food has simply changed location, and eventually through the action of body fluids it will change state. However, it existed, and still exists, albeit in a different form. Matter can neither be created nor destroyed. This is a physical law that is indisputable. You cannot reduce something that exists into nothing, or no-thing (absolute nonexistence). You cannot banish it from physicality; all you can do is alter its state of existence. You cannot create matter; all you can do is alter its nature—either physically or by using the principles of Magic. Nothing exists, in its own right, and is unalterable, yet everything that does exist has come from nothing in the first place.

The three bands of nonexistence are:

Ain = is absolute nonexistence, not even potential, zero, zero, zero.

Ain Soph = is infinite potential, zero, zero.

Ain Soph Aur = is endless empty space, that came from the infinite potential, zero.

The way to understand the zero sphere is to imagine it as the sphere of pure potential—untapped, undisturbed, and unrecognized. It exists, but it is not yet realized. Its practical application, however, is enormous. The nearer we get to zero, or stillness, the nearer we are to that potential. Compare this approach with the more popular pursuit of cavorting around in a plastic circle. Every ritual should start by using the power of still-ness, hence the ideas given to you about pre-ritual relaxation and the common concept of peace and power. During the high point of a ritual, when we are directly instructing the subconscious mind, it is important to push aside all distracting thoughts and feelings, which get in the way of stillness. The more we relax, the more we approach stillness, and the better the result. The same can be said about meditation and contemplation. Stillness, or the ability to reach nothingness, is the way to true power. It is fitting that the zero sphere should be the sphere before the Tree of Life.

Kether-Uranus

The first sphere on the Tree of Life is Kether, the sphere of origins and beginnings. How does anything begin? Quite simply it begins in the mind as a thought, and by thought I mean original thought, the type of thinking that is uniquely yours and belongs to no one else. There is a world of difference between conscious thoughts, in other words thinking *about* something, and pure *original* thought. This type of thinking is difficult to describe. It has to be observed and understood if you are to gain the full value of the Kether. Every new invention, piece of music, and line of poetry is the direct result of original thought. Everyone has this capacity, but few use it, thereby robbing themselves of the opportunity to be themselves. Kether is the sphere of being.

To be yourself and realize your full potential, you must strive to be original. Now can you see why the search for the real self is so important? At best, most humans are a poor reflection of everyone else's ideas. Confused and blind, they desperately try to make this image real with predictable consequences. All failure and lack in life is largely due to this fact. It is inescapable.

Accept nothing without thinking about it first. It was by looking upward at our own galaxy, the Milky Way, that humankind really began to think about its place in the universe and its relationship with the stars. As yet there was no order or discernible pattern, but there was the beginning of many ideas and postulations. Original thinking was being applied—something had caused these stars to appear, and that something was deemed to be God. Later on, humankind was to discover that God also lay within their own being.

From a purely practical point of view, the sphere of Kether should be used in all self-searching operations. It will prove to be of the utmost value for finding who you are and what you are capable of. In addition to using a visual image of galaxies of stars, you can use other attributions, such as a single point. All lines and geometric shapes emanate from a single point. The Chaos Star is a good example of this (see figure 9, below).

Figure 9. The Chaos Star. A singularity with eight arrows symbolizing lines and geometric shapes emanating from the single source.

Just as the sphere of Kether indicates beginnings, so does the Chaos Star symbolize the beginning of manifestation and creation. The Chaos Star represents the singularity of the big bang, which manifested from a point source. This can also be seen from a more mystical-religious-metaphysical viewpoint in the Bible. "And God said, let there be light: and there was light" (Gen. 1:3). The light is the vast explosion of the big bang, when everything exploded in all directions at once. The Chaos Star symbolizes this point of beginning, and its eight arrows depict the act of creation going out in all directions.

Kether belongs to Uranus. The planet Uranus symbolizes the powers of intuition and original thought. Uranus also indicates how a person will deviate from the norm in a birth chart, and its aspects will tell if a person will be constructive and inventive or if he or she will be eccentric and disruptive.[1] In any case, it shows how such a person will exert his or her ability to be different. One further attribution of Uranus is the Crown, which is placed on the head of every true king or queen. Such a king or queen would rule their land with power drawn from the ability to be original and from the ability to be self-motivated in the truest sense of the word. A person set apart from the common herd by right.

Chockmah-Neptune

At the head of the right-hand pillar of the Tree is sphere 2, Chockmah: the pillar of positive action and the idea of the universal father. Potential has now become polarized into male and female, and in Chockmah we are dealing with the former. It should always be understood that humankind is a mixture of male and female. There is no such thing as total male or total female on planet Earth. Kether represents power, movement, and activity. Chockmah represents power being directed along a specific course. The single point has become a straight line or circle. The random patterns of galaxies have now resolved into the structure of the Zodiac.

The planet Neptune is given to Chockmah. Neptune rules our ability to be inspired, and inspiration carries with it a quality of emotion that

---

[1] Maxine Taylor, *Now That I've Cast It, What Do I Do With It?* (MaxineTaylor.com Independently published, 1975).

uplifts the soul. Humankind was inspired by the order contained in the stars to do great things and forge ahead using power free from restrictions. How often have you heard of an inspired work or act? It is the Neptune ability within us. Neptune can raise you to the heights of inspired thoughts and actions or it can lose you in the maze of unreality and over-idealistic impracticalities. Always there is a choice, and the right choice is based on the *wisdom* of correctly applied power. The original idea has now become a dynamic force flowing through correct channels. However, power without a target and without form is of no value, so we must look at the next sphere on the opposing pillar to continue on this journey to physicality.

Binah-Saturn

Sphere 3 is named Binah and is the natural domicile of the Great Mother. The Great Mother gives birth and implies limitation. It is for this reason that Saturn is given to this sphere. Neptune is fluidity, Saturn is solidity. The key word of Binah is understanding, and it is regrettable that Saturn is so little understood, being classified as the great malefic. Without limitation you would not have form, there would be impossible situations, and you would have neither a body nor anything to stand on. The lesson of Binah is "all is as it should be." In other words, if you originate discordant and destructive ideas at Kether, these will find power and possible further confusion at Chockmah and then will eventually find form as restriction in Binah. You as a human being are responsible for who you are and all that manifest around you without exception. The truth of the matter is that you create your own troubles and experience the negative effects of Saturn. No one else is responsible. The reverse is also true; originate from true self-seeking, wise ways and you will achieve perfect results. The law of cause and effect ceases to be a curse, and burdens become achievements, due to understanding. As a further point of contact and contemplation, your straight line or circle has become a triangle of three equal sides. The more astute of you will have noticed that the minimum number of three supports is necessary to produce a stable structure, for a table with only two legs is bound to fall over.

Chesed-Jupiter

Sphere 4 is named Chesed and is the sphere of abundance. It is also the home of Jupiter, the planet of joy, wealth, and opportunity for expansion. The position of this planet in a birth chart will indicate how that person is likely to receive or be denied these benefits, but as always *choice* is the keyword. Everyone has this point of contact with abundance, yet few realize its potential, due to the wrong choice. If you are not experiencing lasting abundance do not blame fate or class yourself as unlucky, this is not true. Abundance exists for everyone; all you have to do is find the key to unlock the door.

Chesed is expansion in every sense of the word and expansion implies a free and unrestricted flow. When you are truly attuned to Chesed, you can never want for anything; you are secure because abundant supply will always exceed the apparent lack. Envy and greed similarly point to a complete lack of understanding of reality. Wanting to have what someone else has is the wrong approach, and it distracts your thinking. If you wish to become rich, then never begrudge the rich their wealth; instead, use this to inspire you to be wealthy—not in exactly the same way, but in your own way. Think rich, think wealth, think abundance.

Remember, ask and it will be given. Nothing will ever be denied if you ask and believe in the laws abundance. Depend on these laws and trust your inner powers of plenty, then allow this power to flow. Remember that you are dealing with the principle of generosity and that this works both ways. A wise person can be truly generous, for they will never fear lack—there is no such thing.

Geburah-Mars

Geburah is the sphere of energy and action. Wasted or out of control energy is usually due to lack of understanding. It results in anger, unwanted force, antagonism, and even war. To every action there is an equal and opposite reaction, according to the laws of physics, and this is true on all levels. Life's energies should produce action along the right paths, provided that you think first and then act.

Mars is the planet of Geburah, and Martian energy needs and implies control, for every action must cause a result. Better to plan and organize, rather than being impulsive, for we are always responsible for our actions, be they in the mind or in physical terms. Cause and effect are little understood, so we give useless excuses to cover up our lack of control, or we have a convenient get-out clause so that we can blame something or somebody else, usually the gods, fate, destiny, or if you really want to indulge in passing the buck, karma. The latter excuse is now an accepted belief pattern by millions of people who have not even thought about the concept, who have failed to realize the true implication of what they are believing in. Any problems are truly yours; you cause them in the same way that you are now learning how to cause far better things to happen. Thinking is the cause. Wrong thinking produces undesirable effects. Change your thinking and you are bound to change your life for the better. The key to the energies of Geburah is stop, think, and then act in a responsible manner.

Tiphereth-Sun

From Geburah we return to the middle pillar, the sphere of Tiphereth and the power of the Sun. Its symbol is the six pointed star, which consists of two perfectly interlaced triangles. The figure suggests *balance* and the *harmony* of opposites, the keywords of this sphere. Tiphereth is right at the heart of the Tree and is connected to every other sphere (except Malkuth). Just as the Sun is at the center of our solar system, so Tiphereth is the center or nervous system of the Tree. It is in this sphere that we must seek to be what we will, in other words, be ourselves while drawing on the energies of all the other spheres. Those who seek knowledge of the central ego and self should always look toward Tiphereth

Balance and harmony are correct life expressions. A far cry from reality, most of life's tragedies and inner conflicts are due to trying to be something that we are not. Be yourself and all else will fall into place in perfect harmony. Again, the concept of right thinking must be applied, for to indulge in negative and non-balanced thinking is to go against what you really are. So not only do you get the results of such thoughts you also produce a clash of interests with resulting inner tension. By seeking within, by using your subconscious power correctly, you restore the balance and you become yourself.

All natural healing of unbalanced conditions belongs to this sphere, for what is disease and discomfort but a lack of balance? The solar energies restore balance by adjusting the energy patterns so that they once again conform to the way you should be. Apart from healing, whatever is put into the subconscious mind will become a reality. By seeking the truth about what you are and what you need, so shall you have all that is right and proper. A popular misconception is to view yourself as a type, for instance:" I am a Sagittarian" or "I am nervous." If you tell yourself these things often enough, you will become these things. Fortunately, choice can always be exercised, and the process is reversed. Therefore, Tiphereth embraces all that you may become, so it is a mistake to narrow the field of possibilities and restrict the self in these ways. Use Tiphereth as your sphere of guidance.

Netzach-Venus

Sphere 7 is named Netzach and contains those energies attributed to Venus. In Cabalistic lore it is named "Victory," a strange name to associate with the planet of peace and love; at first glance you would think that this world be attributed to Mars. So we should look a little deeper. Netzach is the sphere of attraction and desire power. Popular misconception may suggest that you should gain victory over your desires. This is simply incorrect—on the one hand, such a victory would be oppressive, which is hardly Venusian, and on the other hand, you can no more turn off desire power than you can stop breathing permanently. It is the victory over misdirected desires that is important. To desire is not wrong; it is what you desire that matters. There is victory in attracting into your life all those beautiful things you wish to have. There is victory in replacing lust with love, and there is victory in achieving or having the unobtainable. To stoke up the fires of desire power is to want with all your heart. The real victory is to desire all the things that you wish to have purified of all harmful ideas. You can have whatever you desire but take care not to do this in the wrong emotional or mental state.

To desire money is not wrong, but to be greedy or desire someone else's money is wrong. The energy is being misdirected, and the laws of abundance have not been realized. Likewise it's wrong to desire another person without consideration of the other person's needs and feelings. Life is ruled by give and take and sharing. You cannot force someone else to love you or conform to your ideas. True love is binding because the laws of attraction complement each other. Anything else is just a poor compromise. Rituals for love often fail for this reason, for it is not love that is being sought, it is invariably control over someone else. Far better to seek lasting love in pastures new than to try to force another being to conform to an unobtainable ideal. The laws of Netzach teach give and take, rather like a flower. A flower needs to have its seeds fertilized, so it attracts insects by giving color, scent, and honey. So it is with humans; we attract in proportion to what we give out. If you express disharmony and greed, you attract these into your life. Purify your emotions and feelings and use desire power to bring into your life all those things you really need. Such is the lesson of Netzach.

Hod-Mercury

Sphere 8 is named Hod, and its planet is Mercury, the "messenger" of the gods." Mercury rules communication, the way you speak and think, and it is the planet of the conscious mind. Correctly controlled emotions are essential if desire power is to work, and in this sphere you have to learn how to use the mind as a tool for achievement.

 The conscious mind is a tool. In the right hands it is a tool for learning and applying that knowledge for advancement. It can be a source of trouble, complaints, and utter confusion if it is rigidly educated to the wrong standard set by the self, because it is then at variance with the self. When used to plan, compare, examine, and make decisions around the needs of the self, it is functioning correctly, as a tool instead of an encumbrance. The ability to think and then direct the subconscious mind is magical, but the need to indulge in book learning is largely self-defeating unless such a person has no other aims in life.

There is nothing wrong with knowledge if it can be applied or if it satisfies a need, but it is the ability to think in simple terms that gets results, and that is what matters. It is essential to control the mind by seeking peace and then direct it into the appropriate channel. In other words, a mind full of confusion, darting about from one fact to another, will not produce concrete results or influence the subconscious mind beneficially. A quiet, orderly mind concentrating on the objective enables you to plan out your campaign of action and helps you to sort out the wheat from the chaff in magical terms. As you think, so you are. Quiet, calm, contemplative thinking gets results.

Yesod-Moon

Much has been said and written about the Moon and its magical lore, probably because the Moon rules our imagination. I will not duplicate effort in the matter, but rather concentrate on the more useful magical possibilities. There are three paradigms in which the subconscious mind may be influenced: Thinking, which is sphere 8, Hod-Mercury; emotional desire, which is sphere 7, Netzach-Venus; and the power of the imagination, which belongs to sphere 9, Yesod-Moon. The best plan of action is to use all three in proportion to your needs and abilities. Some prefer to use the mind, and they are classified as Hermetic or inhibitory; others prefer to stoke up the emotions, and they are classified as Orphic or excitatory. By themselves neither of these will get results. You have to use some blend and you have to use the imagination. You have to see in your mind's eye what you want, or nothing can happen. For the language of the subconscious is in pictures and symbols.

Yesod and the Moon also govern our response to life and our habits, so it naturally follows that progress is made when you discard those habits that are unproductive or bad. This area of life is well worth a study in its own right, and you will be surprised just how habitual you really are. One of the keys to getting results is knowing that when new thought becomes habit, it works automatically. The lesson is plain to see: Change your thinking, encourage new more desirable habits, and everything changes for the better, staying this way automatically.

Malkuth-Earth

Malkuth is both the sphere in which we start our upward search for perfection and the sphere in which we experience physicality. All previous spheres find expression in Malkuth, so it stands to reason that if there is imbalance in these spheres, the result will automatically be undesirable conditions on the physical plane. Humankind instinctively looks skyward for inspiration and answers to its problems. We look to the stars and to the gods for help. In a way, people are right to look upward, for the problem exists in higher spheres, but not as karma or the anger of extra-terrestrial beings or UFO-related entities. It exists in the misdirected energy patterns within the spheres of the Tree of Life. These are not external to us, they are part of us, for each of us are our own Tree.

The lesson of Malkuth is therefore quite simple—outer conditions are the result of inner thinking, and therefore the solution to the problem is within the problem itself. Not only is Malkuth equivalent to the physical world, it is also that idealistic state we visualize as the Inner Temple. Its symbols are the Encircled Cross, the double cube, and the four elemental gateways of power. Through these doorways we contact and use the power of the Tree of Life and allow that power to produce physical results. The whole of the Tree of Life rests in Malkuth and finds its earthly fulfillment therein. To work effective Magic we must start at Malkuth and its Inner Temple, opening these doorways to the vast storehouse of power available from the rest of the Tree. Unless this sphere is organized, understood, and worked with in a sensible fashion, physical results will either be unrewarding (at best) or unchangeable (at worst). By building up the Inner Temple along correct symbolic lines, we form stable ground for the rest of the Tree to grow and bear fruit.

Daath-Pluto

There is a barrier between the power of Daath and yourself—that barrier is fear. Nothing prevents growth more than fear. Always remember, in reality there is nothing to fear except fear itself. By fear I do not mean the normal protective fear we experience during moments of danger; I mean unfounded fear, fear of God, fear of the unknown, fear of pushing ahead because it might not work, and so on. You have the power to do anything, to be whatever you want to be, to have whatever you wish; let no one tell you otherwise. Results depend on positive thinking and belief in what you are doing; fear destroys creation before we can even start. When you beat fear you acquire much more than the power to create; you acquire self-determination and total freedom from the imaginary demons that plague humankind. To seek the power of Daath and its planet Pluto you will have to overcome these fears and taboos. The path is not easy, but you can succeed if you are determined enough. The solution to a fear is like a problem, within the fear itself; once beaten, you are unafraid and nothing can stand in your way.

Daath-Pluto contains the power to transform your life. By beating fear, superstition, and taboos and by shining light into the darkest corners of your mind, you will experience this transformation. In ancient times an initiate was put through fearsome tests and ordeals to see if they had the necessary qualities expected of such a person. Today's initiations contain a poor reflection of this idea. Facing up to and beating fear is vital to self-development, although we no longer need the lion's den or the pit of fire. We need to search within for the cause of fear, and use the power of Daath to shine the powerful light of cosmic truth onto these causes and see them for what they are. Light always illuminates darkness, and so it is with Daath. Once a thing is in full view, we can see it and understand it, thereby equating it and eventually transforming it. To live is to be free and to be free is the reality of life. The Tree of Life is your plan of freedom.

Summary of the Tree of Life

Below is a summary of the important principles of the Tree of Life. It explains the essential information that you should not forget. After you have carefully read this chapter, try to recall as many of the outstanding points as you can.

At the top of the Tree we have sphere 1, named Kether. It represents the beginning of something and so equates with originality and individuality. It is the sphere of new ideas. As this is the first sphere, all the others emanate from and are contained within it. It contains all there is, and as such it represents pure potential. At the physical end it is best represented by the planet Uranus. A photograph of the galaxy will give you a perfect idea of the allness and dynamic power that is Kether. Its symbol is a Crown. As for color, while white is traditional I prefer to use transparency, rather like clear glass, for although Kether contains all the colors they are not as yet manifest.

Sphere 2 is named Chockmah; its keyword is *wisdom,* and it represents the All-Father principle. From a physical point of view its planet is Neptune and its color is pure white, or you may wish to use grey (pearl grey, iridescent). The Zodiac also fits well into this sphere, for is not the science of the stars nothing more than pure wisdom?

With sphere 3 we move to the opposite pillar and the Great Mother. This sphere is named Binah. Its color is pure black, and its ruling planet is Saturn. It may seem strange that the apparently restrictive planet Saturn should equate to a mother, but remember that in its correct aspect Saturn is the planet that gives form, and birth is the giving of form. The keyword for this sphere is *understanding.*

Back on the right-handed pillar once more we arrive at sphere 4, Chesed, the color blue, and the planet Jupiter. Here we are dealing with limitless and abundant expansion in keeping with the idea of the fortune-bestowing god of the vine. The keyword is *mercy,* but please do not confuse this with the version dished out by Christianity. This sphere represents pure mercy, free from religious overtones.

In direct opposition we have sphere 5, named Geburah. Its color is red and its planet is Mars. The keywords are *justice* and *might.* Like Saturn, Mars often has a bad reputation because it rules aggression and war (among other things); however, always remember that although everything fits on the Tree, it is far better to exclude negative attributions and seek the positive possibilities instead. If you lose your temper, you ruin your chances of controlling power by losing control and thereby dissipating that power. This sphere therefore represents energy, enterprise, and initiation.

On the middle pillar we arrive at sphere 6, named Tiphereth. Look at its position. It is central to the whole Tree; therefore, like the center of the solar system, it becomes the light within your inner self (in human terms). Middle pillar spheres are too abstract to have colors; however, the colors yellow or preferably gold may be used. The keywords are *beauty* and *harmony.*

Our next sphere is number 7. Its name is Netzach and its planet Venus. Its color is emerald green. Venus is the principle of attraction. It is our personal magnetism that helps us bring into fruition the nicer things in our lives. *Victory,* which is the keyword of this sphere, may at first seem quite odd until we realize that by controlling our emotions and redirecting them as desire power we are bound to gain victory over circumstances.

Sphere 8 is named Hod; its planet is Mercury (the symbol of the mind), and its color is orange. Mercury rules communication—the way you speak and think. The major lesson you can learn from Mercury is to reorganize your thinking into simple, realistic patterns, moving away from the more chaotic forms of the accepted norm. The training of the mind is an essential part of all real Magic. *Flexibility, adaptability,* and *communication* are the words of this sphere.

Sphere 9 on the middle pillar is named Yesod, its color is silver, and its planet is the Moon. The Moon is responsible for our imagination—that powerful magical tool that gives us access to the subconscious mind represented by Tiphereth. By using the imagination, we shape all that is around us. Little wonder that the keyword—*foundation*—is so apt. We have the ability to build whatever we wish in whatever way we wish in our imagination.

Finally, we reach sphere 10, Malkuth, and this is the Earth sphere. The end product of all that has gone before, magically, it is the sphere of the four elements. By using these elements we apply power to physical matter and shape this according to our needs. Malkuth is our ideal world in addition to being the Inner Temple, yet another idealistic state of existence in which we work all meaningful magical rituals. The difference between the ideal world of Malkuth and planet Earth is blatantly obvious to everyone. There is a world of difference, yet the secret of Malkuth is in bringing the ideal into physical fact. Such is Magic on a practical level, for Malkuth is in reality the sphere of practicality. With regard to colors, there are of course four, one for each element. These are yellow for Air and east, red for Fire and south, blue for Water and west, and green for Earth and north.

The Position of the Spheres

When thinking about the spheres, bear in mind their position. For instance with sphere 4, Chesed, we have the expansion of Jupiter, with the underlying tone of the right-hand pillar, in other words, positive out flowing with generous and kind emotions. Or with sphere 5, Geburah, the use of energy based on our ability to receive it using the power of the mind. Look at the diagram of Tree of Life in this chapter (figure 6, page 79); read this chapter many times; and think about the spheres, the number, and the ideas given to you.

Relating these to the Cosmic Sphere is not difficult. Sphere 1, Kether, belongs to the uppermost point, while sphere 10, Malkuth, belongs to the base. This fits in well with the age-old idea of God above and man below or, put in practical terms, initial power and final product.

Sphere 2 is likely to give most Cabalistic thinkers something of a problem; however, this is solved by giving the entire outer structure to this sphere. The reason is simple if you remember that, although the ruling planet is Neptune, the other main attribution of Chockmah is the Zodiac, which, in turn, implies the idea of the three rings.

We are now left with seven spheres, excluding Daath. These belong to the faces of the Magic Cube, using the ruling planets. For example sphere 8, Hod, equates to the eastern face of the cube, while sphere 6, Tiphereth, naturally belongs to the center. Here we have a perfect scheme. In the center is the Sun, around which are arrayed the planets. The whole of this magical solar system is, as one would expect, surrounded by the stars in the form of the Zodiac. All that remains is to locate that enigmatic sphere of Daath. Despite the ideas and taboos found in other sources of information. Daath, together with its Pluto ruler, equate to transformation that leads to ultimate power and total realization. The myth of the Phoenix affords valuable clues as to the correct location in that this mythological bird is consumed by fire in order to be reborn. This, together with the vast power potential of Pluto, must mean that Daath is to be found at the center also, within the Sun.

The Hexagram

As you have come to observe, symbol diagrams are inevitably a flat representation of a three-dimensional reality. The simple Encircled Cross is representative of the Cosmic Sphere, and now the Tree of Life can be seen to be an extension of this scheme. As a student of Esoteric Magic, you should look at all other symbols in this light, for there is much to be gained and learned from symbols.

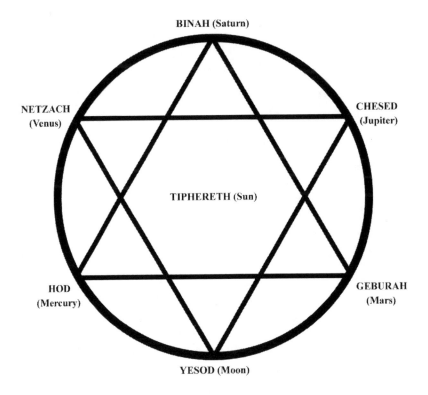

Figure 10. The Hexagram.

The Hexagram, so beloved of the Golden Dawn, is yet another plan of a three-dimensional configuration. Do you know what this is? Consider figure 10 carefully.

Note that there are six points. What does this suggest? The answer is the Cube (six faces). There are other clues, some of which are to be found in the Tree diagram. That is, provided that you allow this to be flexible. Notice the arrangement of spheres (and planets) around the center of the Tree (Tiphereth-Sun).

HOD (Mercury) is opposite to CHESED (Jupiter)
NETZACH (Venus) is opposite to GEBURAH (Mars)
BINAH (Saturn) is opposite to YESOD (Moon)

This, of course, agrees with our conception of the magical cube. If you now look at the Hexagram, adding the appropriate spheres and planets, you will see that not only does it agree with the cube plan but the Tree of Life as well. The Hexagram is therefore a flat representation of the Cube (see figure 11, page 108), or Inner Temple.

Also notice that the Tree of Life constantly suggests the idea of polarity. This can be seen not only in the pillars but in many other areas as well. Look again at the Cube and Hexagram. Mercury-Hod is representative of the conscious mind, while Jupiter-Chesed equates to the deeper mind. They are both connected with the mind but from a different point of view. Likewise, Venus-Netzach and its associations with attraction, desire, and female qualities is exactly balanced by the male-dominated power of Mars-Geburah. The essential part of this idea is one of balance. This is indicated quite clearly by the middle pillar and the sphere of Tiphereth, which is central to the entire Tree design. You will also note that Tiphereth (Sun) is also placed at the central balancing power of the Cube.

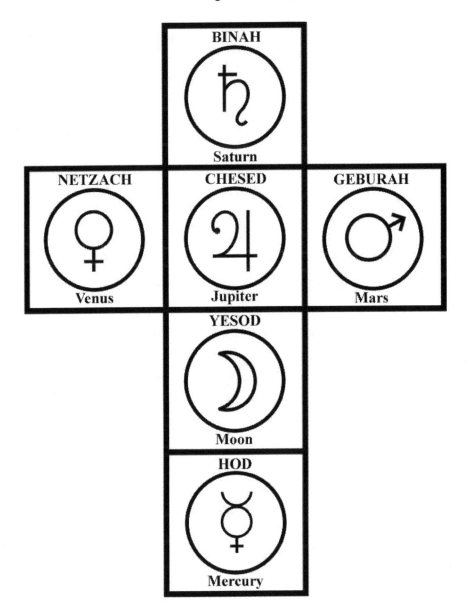

Figure 11. The Magic Cube.

Familiarizing Yourself
With the Tree Diagram

Continue with your work on the planets. The information gained will be of value to helping you understand the Tree in a personal sense, for each planet relates directly to a sphere. Familiarize yourself with the Tree diagram. Make sketches or draw the Tree of Life carefully onto a card. This may be used as a point of concentration during subsequent ritual work. Color the spheres using crayon, poster paint, or felt-tip pens. Obviously, it is impossible to use transparent ink for Kether or ultraviolet for Daath, so these may be left blank and the actual color presumed for the time being. In keeping with good magical practice, get involved with this simple task, take your time and use your ingenuity to create a *personal* Tree diagram you can be proud of. The more you put in, the more you get out.

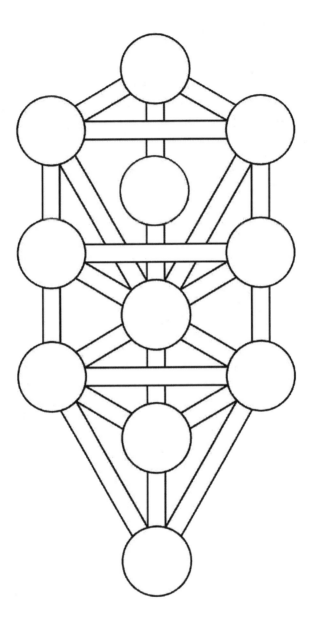

Figure 12. Blank Tree of Life.

How to Erect and Attune to Each Sphere

In order to make use of the Tree of Life, it is essential that a realistic approach be used, free from over complexity, incorrect attributions, and other nonrelated ideals. It is also essential that the Tree paradigm be *personal* rather than general. Only by adopting a personal approach can the Tree truly reveal its meaning.

There are many misconceptions concerning the Tree of Life, and perhaps the greatest is the idea that this is a sort of ladder that has to be climbed in order to evolve. Belief patterns such as this do nothing for the art and practice of Magic and are, in any case, completely false. The only real evolution is one of ridding ourselves of such self-restrictive ideas. Forget about evolving and accept the more correct concept that you are evolved. This is most important, for failure to realize this truth is bound to limit your life and, of course, restrict the possibilities offered by the Tree. One example of this is the presumption that the supernals (spheres 1, Kether; 2, Chockmah; and 3, Binah) are not accessible to the student. They are presumed to be beyond him or her. This is absolute rubbish and is based on the outmoded system of grades advocated by the Order of the Golden Dawn. In this system, the novice was initiated into each sphere, gradually climbing the Tree as the Order saw fit. The higher the sphere, the more difficult the task—or so we are lead to believe. Naturally, the higher spheres were reserve for individuals of rare talent and powerful abilities. Let us forget all about rising up the Tree by means of grades and meaningless initiations. Instead, we will use the Tree as it is meant to be used—as a plan of potential and a means of self-discovery.

The Tree consists of ten spheres (eleven with Daath). Each is different, being a specific categorization of energy, and each contains its own inner truths directly relating to the individual. In order to gain access to the knowledge of a sphere and, of course, to the power therein, it is essential that you learn how to erect each sphere and how to equate to it meaningfully. Not an easy task if you believe traditional sources. Fortunately, the task is not as difficult as you would think; in fact it is quite easy, provided that certain guidelines are followed.

Each sphere, by its very nature, is a three-dimensional configuration rather than the convenient flat circle given in the Tree diagram. You work *within* this rather than on it or outside it. Also, although the Tree of Life shows these spheres as being separate, connected by paths, this is not strictly true and can easily lead the student to presume that the spheres are in fact separated by space. By far the best way of looking at the spheres is to ignore the way in which they are spread out, for this is only a convenient way of representing a complex arrangement. Instead, adopt the idea of one structure in which all the others may be found, rather like a room with different colored windows or perhaps a house containing several rooms. The main structure has already been given to you. It is the Cosmic Sphere of three rings. This equates to the lowest sphere on the Tree of Life, known as Malkuth or the Kingdom. Malkuth is the sphere of the four elements and the ideal world. Let us examine this in a little more detail.

The Cosmic Sphere, which we will refer to as Malkuth from now on, contains everything. Therefore, the entire Tree of Life may be found within its structure. This has already been discussed in the previous chapter in which the spheres were allocated to the nodal points and to the inner cube. The Tree of Life symbol is a flat representation of this three-dimensional structure, which, in turn, is the Cosmic Sphere of Malkuth.

Malkuth is the sphere in which all Practical Magic is worked. Note how this is done by using an assortment of words, gestures, symbols, and physical objects backed up with the power of the imagination to help attune the mind to the task in hand and, of course, the energy being use.

The accent is on contacting or attuning to a specific type of energy, usually epitomized as planetary. What are we actually doing other than bringing this energy into our consciousness? We do not travel to a planet or to some remote part of ourselves to do this; we allow it to flow by recognizing that it exists and thereby allowing it into our life. This process can easily be seen in the flat Tree diagram in which the entire Tree of Life impacts, or finds fruition, in the base sphere Malkuth. That is the function of this sphere—to act as a point of impact for energy. Before energy can flow, we must first recognize it, using symbols and so forth, and then allow it to flow into our life. In Malkuth this is done by attuning this sphere to the energy required and then allowing this to enter into the sphere of Malkuth through the four elemental gateways.

The sphere of Malkuth can therefore be attuned to anything that lies above it—in short, the entire Tree of Life! To do this is not difficult, but it does, like all magical work, need some consideration and practice before it can be truly effective. We will consider this attunement in a moment but, for now, let us return to Malkuth itself.

Before your magical work can be effective, it is essential that the Cosmic Sphere be constructed carefully and practiced until it is second nature. After all, if the base sphere is somewhat shaky, then one can hardly expect the rest of the Tree to be stable. Trees need roots in deep fertile earth lest they blow over or starve. It is the same with Malkuth.

The better the base sphere, the better the Tree scheme. So resist the temptation to rush ahead hoping to find shortcuts to knowledge or presuming that Malkuth, being the lowest of the spheres, is hardly worth any detail consideration. This would be a prime mistake, for Malkuth is the key to the entire Tree and the only real gateway to power.

You have been given many useful ideas with regard to the sphere of Malkuth. These should be worked with and extended in any way that you feel is right, for personal involvement is a major factor in successful mastery of Magic and the Tree of Life. By all means use these ideas to the fullest, but do remember that it is your own ideas that will ultimately prove to be the best. Be guided by *feel,* and do not be afraid to try out new ideas. It is better to try, even if you do make mistakes, than not to try at all. Keep a magical notebook in which to record any impressions or ideas received either during meditations or at any other times. Be methodical and practical; it is bound to pay off in the end.

Attuning the sphere to Malkuth (as opposed to consideration of the entire sphere) is a simple affair, provided that certain rules are followed. These rules apply equally to all other spheres. First must come clear intention. In other words, know which sphere you are working. This may sound obvious, but all too often there is presumption rather than assertion. A clear well-thought-out intention is a major key to successful Practical Magic and is no less so in esoteric matters. Once the intention is clear, organize the temple in such a way as to enhance this purpose. Bring in the appropriate correspondences to help focus the mind along the chosen path or energy patterns. In the case of Malkuth, this would mean bringing in those objects that will serve to remind us of the nature of this sphere.

Before you start to purchase masses of equipment or clutter the temple up with all manner of attributions to be found, stop and think. *Simplicity* is always the best way to get results. In fact, one or two well-chosen items are bound to be far more effective than a whole host of odds and ends acquired from dubious sources. Take nothing into a temple unless it is understood. Sound advice indeed.

With this sphere, you are mainly dealing with the four elements. These may be represented by the four weapons or their equivalent. Do remember that it is not vital to purchase, say, a Magic Sword. These things cost a small fortune. Instead, use a substitute such as a small knife or dagger. This may be personalized according to your needs. Alternatively, it is possible to obtain inexpensive reproduction swords or find real swords in second hand shops at moderate prices. It is not the cost, or indeed the shape and size that matters at this stage. All that you are looking for, in this case, is a symbolic representation of the element of Air. Think about this. Use your imagination and apply that all-important personal touch, even if the ideal Magic Sword is not at hand.

A Magic Rod or Wand should be made. Again, use your imagination to determine what you would like to see as a representation of the element of Fire. By thinking in this way, you are bound to arrive at a succession of designs that will teach you far more than simply coping something out of a book. Magic Cups can also be purchased quite cheaply. They can be made of metal or even glass. Once again, it is all a question of choice, based on your own thoughts. Finally, the Magic Shield should be made by yourself using metal, wood, or even stiff card. The design is very important. Forget about Pentagrams and other trendy designs. What do you think should be emblazoned on the Shield? When you have decided on this, find some way of transferring this design onto the Shield. There are many ways. Felt-tip pen or poster paints are among some of the possibilities. Also remember that it really does not matter if you have an artistic touch or not. What does matter is that you try in your own way to reproduce the ideas in your own mind. To try is to succeed, no matter what others may think, and, in any case, any sincere, original effort is worth a thousand imitations or copies made without so much as a second thought.

The Tarot

Perhaps the most versatile and useful of all magical tools is the tarot. Although it is not the purpose of this book to enter into detailed discussion of this intricate system, I will advance a few useful ideas that you, the student, may care to expand in your own ways. Tarot cards fit the

Cabalistic scheme with a precision that cannot be described as accidental. In brief, the seventy-eight cards are divided into twenty-two *major* cards and fifty-six *minor* cards. The major cards belong to the paths that are discussed in the next chapter. For now, we will confine ourselves to the minor cards only.

The minor cards are divided into four suits of fourteen cards. Naturally, each suit equates to one of the four elements. Leaving aside the court cards (Kings, Queens, Knights, and Pages); we are left with forty cards, ten for each suit or element. It is the number that gives the clue to the correct arrangement on the Tree of Life. The suit indicates the correct magical direction by its weapon and element. For instance, the 10 of Swords belong to Malkuth (sphere 10) and the east (Swords). Likewise, the 8 of Cups belong to Hod (sphere 8) and to magical west (Cups).

The complete arrangement of the minor cards is given in the following table:

SPHERE	EAST	SOUTH	WEST	NORTH
	Swords	Wands	Cups	Shields
Kether	Ace	Ace	Ace	Ace
Chockmah	2	2	2	2
Binah	3	3	3	3
Chesed	4	4	4	4
Geburah	5	5	5	5
Tiphereth	6	6	6	6
Netzach	7	7	7	7
Hod	8	8	8	8
Yesod	9	9	9	9
Malkuth	10	10	10	10

No tarot card represents Daath.

To use the tarot in Cabalistic work is quite an easy matter, for it lends itself easily to this. In the case of Malkuth, the four 10s could be placed on the altar, aligned to their respective directions, or could be placed on the appropriate wall or quarter within the temple. They may be used as symbols for contemplation or as astral doorways through which one passes in the imagination. The scene depicted on a card may then be explored to see what impressions arise in the mind. Other ideas include their use as an on/off switch for each element. In order to do this, one has only to educate the conscious mind in the basic idea that face up opens the elemental gate while face down closes it. Ingenuity will suggest other uses.

In order to attune the Cosmic Sphere to another sphere, one simply has to change the physical correspondences and, of course, the inner, imaginative associations. The correspondences of a particular sphere are the subject of much debate and heated exchanges, but this need not interfere with your work, for most of these attributions are, to say the least, highly dubious. Far better to apply common sense and simplicity.

The most obvious link with each sphere is through its ruling planet, and so it is to the correspondences of the planets that you must first turn if you are to successfully contact each sphere.

However, the planet is only part of the picture, one level, so to speak. There are three more.

Each sphere consists of four worlds. According to tradition, these are:

Atziluth   The world of origins, or Divine level (Air—Thought)

Briah   The world of creation, or Archangelic level (Fire—Desire)

Yetzirah   The world of formation, or Angelic level   (Water—Emotion)

Assiah   The world of expression, or Physical level   (Earth—
Physical Object or Situation)

The power of each sphere may therefore be tapped by bringing it
through each of the worlds to its ultimate fruition in Assiah (the physical). Naturally, each world may be explored and approached directly, for,
despite opinions to the contrary, there are no barriers between you and a
particular level—all are open to you. But how to approach, understand,
and eventually use each level is indeed a complex problem—or so it
seems. Leaving aside pseudo religious attitudes and associated dogma,
the answer, as always, is contained in the Tree of Life.

There are four worlds. These equate directly to the four elements in
the following way: The Divine or God level best belongs to the element
of Air by virtue of the fact that the cosmic circle originates at east *(origi-
nation being the keyword)*. To south and the element of Fire must go the
creative world of Briah. The formative world of Yetzirah belongs to west
and the element of Water and, finally, the north and the element of Earth
belongs to Assiah. Although there are other supposed traditional ar-
rangements, each with their own merits or dogmas, these associations are
correct. Naturally, each student must accept or decline the invitation to
try out this carefully deliberated system.

The erection or attunement of each sphere is best done by attending to
the physical end first, using suitable correspondences and then working
through each of the four levels, either from top to bottom or in reverse,
depending on the nature of the work in hand. Perhaps the easiest way to
describe this is to give an example. Let us consider a meditation of the
sphere of Yesod.

Yesod-Moon Meditation

Gather the appropriate correspondences, in this case those of the Moon. This would involve using silver candles and altar cloth, a mirror (indicative of the reflective Moon), a good lunar incense, and the four 9s of the tarot. Having attended to these preliminaries, all that remains is to open the temple in the manner given in the Master Ritual. The high point of the ritual would be the attunement to Yesod followed by a meditation. This is done in the imagination in the following way:

First, direct your attention to the Crown. This is the symbolic point from which all power flows and also equates to the All-Father. Imagine that the Crown is studded with ten jewels, one for each planet (or sphere) in the appropriate colors. In the case of Yesod, this would be a silver jewel or perhaps a pearl. See this begin to glow with bright silver light and imagine that this is moving downward into the temple. The power must then be allowed into the temple through the four elemental gateways, starting at magical east, the Divine level of Atziluth, and proceeding around the circle, through each level (or world), finally terminating at the magical north (Assiah). By far the best way to do this is by imagining that there is a doorway in each wall of the inner, cubic temple and that, at your command, each one opens allowing the silver light to enter. The exact manner of doing this is largely a matter of choice, but it is always a good idea to bring in the control symbol of the magical weapons. For instance, at magical east, imagine that you are holding the Sword (do this physically if you have a real Sword) and that as you point this at the doorway, it opens.

Suitable words may be spoken as long as they are yours and they do not contain undesirable elements, such as subservience to the gods and so on. Simple statements of fact are the best, such as, "Through this portal, under the control of this Sword, do I contact the [name level] of the sphere of Yesod to make manifest its presence within this temple. May this be so." Short, simple statements of fact are worth far more than any long-winded and half-understood invocation directed at some distant deity or other entity. Deal with power directly until you fully understand the art of building and using telesmatic images. In any case, avoid the traditional images and names, for these are largely corrupt and unusable without considerable modification.

Notice what has been done so far. You have contacted and invoked the positive (All-Father or God) aspect and power descended in a clockwise direction. To balance this out, invoke the negative, or receptive, female (Earth-Mother). Direct your attention to the lower point, as symbolized by the magical Cube, and see this glow with silver light. Allow this light to rise upward. Again, this can be seen to enter the temple through the four gateways, this time in counterclockwise direction, starting at east.

Forget all those silly stories about counterclockwise rotation around the circle being evil or having anything to do with Black Magic or Witchcraft—this is nonsense. Clockwise rotation represents male, counterclockwise represents female. Those unfortunate souls, who leap around their circles in a counterclockwise direction, hoping to contact the Devil, have not even begun to understand the first principles of magical work!

All that remains is to concentrate on the center. There are many ways of doing this. Ingenuity, personal involvement, and practice are bound to suggest good ideas. Here are some ideas that you may care to try out.

The whole point of a magical meditation is to gain useful information that will be of value, not only in magical work but in life as well. There is little point in performing meditations out of some sense of duty or because it seems to be the done thing. Mediate for a purpose. Be pragmatic. In order to remove confusion and, at the same time, gain the maximum amount of relatable information, it is necessary to narrow down your awareness to within definable limits. This is done by continuing to use the correct attributions in the imagination and by confining the meditation to those areas likely to be most productive. In a general sense, the center and the four gateways provide the best means of contacting the reality of sphere and so should be used until other ideas emerge.

The center can be represented by a golden cube, usually in the form of an elaborately carved altar, although there are other variations. By changing the color of this altar to the prime color of the sphere, you have a very potent symbol. Hold this in your mind and then allow ideas to arise around it. It is possible to take this further by adding other compatible symbols that are in keeping with the nature of the sphere under investigation. In the case of Yesod, this could easily be represented as a crescent Moon that lies on or above the altar. Other symbols may also be used. Again, these are all a matter of personal choice.

However, do choose carefully. In particular, do not use the attributions given in books unless you are completely satisfied that these are right for you. Better to keep things simple than to clutter up the mind with a variety of dubious and unrelated symbols that have not been thought through.

The other main area of concentration is that of the four gateways. These may be seen as doorways within the Inner Cubic Temple or as separate temples each containing one of the four weapons. Each separate temple could be explored and is likely to reveal much in terms of esoteric knowledge. In addition, use the symbols of the tarot. Each card, if used within a correctly attuned sphere, will reveal far more than by using any other method. In short, you will see more because your mind is already concentrated along the right line of awareness. Used in conjunction with the gateways, they form an admirable base from which to explore the fascinating realms of the inner mind. They may be seen as actually being on the doors or they may be used as a basic scene into which you enter and subsequently explore. The choice is yours.

Do, however, keep in mind your location within the Cosmic Sphere, for it is quite easy to become lost in associated ideas and side-tracks. This is perhaps the greatest secret of successful meditations, for all too often the novice allows the mind to wander aimlessly, rather than keeping it within the limits needed to produce worthwhile results. There is no need to strain over this. All that is necessary is to use the symbols as controls. For instance, if, during a meditation on Yesod, you are exploring the gateways, keep in mind where you are. This is quite easy, provided that you use the appropriate symbol. With the eastern gateway, you would, of course, limit the awareness to the yellow door of Air, using the symbol of the Sword. Awareness may be narrowed down further by using the sphere attributions. If, for instance, the sphere being worked was Malkuth, then you would bring in additional symbolism to suit this. A good idea would be to see a number ten on this door or perhaps the 10 of Swords. If the sphere was Yesod, you would use the number nine and the 9 of Swords and so on.

By using these ideas and building on them in your own way, you will have a perfect system of self-discovery. Now we will look at an extra dimension that is guaranteed to personalize your work and thereby reveal far more than was previously possible.

Discovering Your
Personal Magical Directions

Here are some useful attributions connected with the four elements. In addition, you will see a list of the ten planets under each element. Now is your chance to get interactive and discover your personal planets and their directions. To find your personal magical directions, you will need a copy of your birth chart.[1] The best way to obtain this is to order your chart calculations from an astrological service. You will then know where the Zodiac signs and planets are placed by studying the Triplicities table in your chart. This will show you how many planets you have ruled by each of the four elements of Air, Fire, Water, and Earth. Then study the aspects table, which will tell you what planets are ruling in what signs. Starting with the first house (Aries) in your birth chart, you will study each house in turn, until you have covered the whole of your chart from Aries through all twelve signs of Taurus, Gemini, Cancer, Leo, Virgo, Libra, Scorpio, Sagittarius, Capricorn, Aquarius, and Pisces.

To begin, find Aries in your chart and see if there are any planets in this sign or house. If there are any planets in this house, then they will all manifest through the south and the element of Fire, For Aries is a Fire sign. This always dictates which magical direction you should work. Now focus on the second house, Taurus, and see if there is a planet or planets in this sign. Then move on to Cancer and so on. If, for example, you were to find more than one planet in a house or sign, all of these planets would manifest through that house's direction and element. I hope you can see the pattern here.

AIR

Symbol: ◯

Magical direction: East

Magical weapon: The Sword

Time of day: Dawn

Time of year: Spring

---

[1] A FREE birth chart may be obtained from https://cafeastrology.com/free-natal-chart-report-equal-houses.html

Zodiac signs: Libra, Aquarius, Gemini
Keywords: Communication
Human associations: Thinking and the realm of mental activity
Tarot card: 10 of Swords

Personal planets ruled by the Sword and the Air element (circle appropriate planet(s) from your birth chart): Sun, Moon, Mercury, Venus, Mars, Jupiter, Saturn, Uranus, Neptune, Pluto

FIRE
Symbol:
Magical direction: South
Magical weapon: The Rod, Wand, or Spear
Time of day: Noon
Time of year: Summer
Zodiac sign: Aries, Leo, Sagittarius
Keyword: Direction
Human association: Desiring and the realm of creative activity
Tarot card: 10 of Wands

Personal planets ruled by the Rod and the Fire element (circle appropriate planet(s) from your birth chart): Sun, Moon, Mercury, Venus, Mars, Jupiter, Saturn, Uranus, Neptune, Pluto

WATER
Symbol:
Magical direction: West
Magical weapon: The Cup, Horn, or Chalice
Time of day: Dusk
Time of year: Autumn

Zodiac signs: Cancer, Scorpio, Pisces

Keyword: Receptivity

Human associations: Feeling and the realm of the emotions

Tarot card: 10 of Cups

Personal planets ruled by the Cup and the Water element (circle appropriate planet(s) from your birth chart): Sun, Moon, Mercury, Venus, Mars, Jupiter, Saturn, Uranus, Neptune, Pluto

EARTH

Symbol: ☐

Magical direction: North

Magical weapon: The Shield

Time of day: Night

Time of year: Winter

Zodiac signs: Capricorn, Taurus, Virgo

Keyword: Having

Human association: Actuality and the realm of physical fact

Tarot card: 10 of Pentacles

Personal planets ruled by the Shield and the Earth element (Circle appropriate planet(s) from your birth chart): Sun, Moon, Mercury, Venus, Mars, Jupiter, Saturn, Uranus, Neptune, Pluto

In Magic, and in life itself, we are constantly dealing with polarity and its various ramifications. The main concern is, however, our relationship with life energies as indicated by the planets and, of course, the ruling sphere. This gives you two ways to look at the matters, for there is *you* and there is *energy*. Both are separate, yet both interact, and through this interaction you create whatever you will. The nature and flow of energies is indicated by the movements of the planets and their interactions in terms of aspects and so forth. It is not the purpose of this work to enter into the complications of this, although it is partly covered in the final chapter. For now, we will concentrate on certain principles that may be used to enhance your magical work.

Each planet has a natural affinity with an element and therefore has a natural magical direction within the Cosmic Sphere.

PLANET	ELEMENT	MAGICAL DIRECTION
Sun	Fire	South
Moon	Water	West
Mercury	Air	East
Venus	Earth	North
Mars	Fire	South
Jupiter	Water	West
Saturn	Earth	North
Uranus	Air	East
Neptune	Water	West
Pluto	Water	West

By equating the planets to the sphere, you can give prime magical directions. These are:

	EAST	SOUTH	WEST	NORTH
Sphere	1, 8	5, 6	2, 4, 9, Daath	3, 7

Malkuth has no prime direction because it contains, and is the receptacle for, all the spheres.

In dealing with cosmic energies as they exist in their own right, it is therefore better to use these directions, due to natural affinity. For example, should you wish to explore the nature of the Sun, you would use the principles given, concentrating and using the prime magical direction of south. In brief, this would consist of focusing the mind on the Crown and allowing golden light to enter the temple starting at magical south, continuing in a clockwise direction. The female (receptive) part of the sphere would be brought into play by focusing the mind on the lower Cube and then allowing golden light to enter the temple, again starting at magical south, in a counterclockwise direction. The sphere is now attuned not only to Tiphereth but to the Sun as it exists as a source of energy outside of yourself. By using this method of attunement, it is possible to explore and understand the planets and ruling spheres in terms of potential.

Power, energy, potential—call it what you will—is, for the sake of simplicity, seen as being "out there" exerting an influence on ourselves and on earthly matter and so on. The opposite side of the coin is the effect that this has on each individual. Every human being has access to power, even though they may not be aware of this. This can be discovered through that person's birth chart and, as far as Esoteric Magic is concerned, it can be resolved into planetary affinities with the four gateways once again. This time, however, the accent and the usage is different, for here we are dealing with the way in which power is accepted by the person.

On pages 123, 124, and 125, you are given lists of planets that are ruled by the directions and the appropriate elements. These are very important because they are taken from your birth chart, which, in turn, is nothing less than a map or plan of your inner potential and abilities. These directions are to be used when attuning the sphere in a personal sense and for any meditations and magical workings involving you rather than pure energy. For example, suppose that you were exploring the sphere of Netzach from a personal point of view, perhaps to discover something about yourself or how this sphere affects your life and so forth. Once again, the procedure of using the upper Crown and the lower Cube in a clockwise and counterclockwise directions would still apply, for these are invariable principles. However, the prime magical direction would be changed from the natural to the personal. For instance, if a student had Venus (the ruling planet of Netzach) ruled by the Air element and the Magic Sword, then the natural magical direction of north would be replaced by east.

The use of the two alternative schemes gives each student even more possibilities, while using natural correspondences in the best possible way. All that you need to remember before starting a meditation is which end of the polarity you are intending to use or explore—you or it. In other words, do you intend to use the sphere in a personal sense, or are you interested in the sphere in its own right? This must always be considered, for all magical work is concerned with either the subjective (self) or the objective (it) approach. As always, you must know what you are doing before you do it.

Naturally, the next question is bound to be, "Can I combine the two?" This will be covered in the next chapter in which we look at the real power of the Tree—the paths.

A Realistic Guide to Pathworking

I have lost count of the number of magically minded people who have never bothered to work with the paths, either through lack of knowledge or basic information or as a result of having succumbed to what must surely add up to propaganda issued by lodges and devotees of dogma. Pathworking, we are told, is an absolute *must* for all serious magical practitioners, yet the manner in which this is taught (and I use the word "taught" loosely) is little better than the absurd practices of spiritualists or those strange limb-twisting exercises practiced by those who subscribe to pseudo-Eastern meditations. Instead of using the paths as clearly defined boundaries within which you may gather specific information, the accent is often more toward "let us see what happens." Real magicians do not open themselves up to random probabilities in this fashion, nor do they adopt what is little better than a hotchpotch of symbolic forms presented by so-called experts, living or dead. Instead, they adopt that much more sane approach of using good techniques and realistic imagery coupled with common sense. Let us look at the paths in detail and then formulate a realistic technique for their exploration and use.

To begin with, the Tree of Life specifies twenty-two paths, but there are far more. Given that everything in existence must be contained within the Tree plan, there is an anomaly between what is actually happening in life and the supposed totality of the Tree. It is this very fact that demands a complete rethinking of the paths.

Let us consider a typical path—path eleven—which lies between sphere 1, Kether, and sphere 2, Chockmah. From a planetary point of view, in other words, the Assiah level, the only true path to actually exist in physical terms, is that created when the two planets are forming an *aspect* in the heavens. Any astrologer will tell you that when an aspect is formed between two (or more) planets there is a flow of energy. The nature of this flow is similar to the combined effects of the planets forming the aspect. Aspects are an astrological and astronomical fact—they happen. Where then, when a planet such as Uranus forms an aspect to the Moon, is the equivalent path on the Tee of Life? Apparently it does not exist! Yet this cannot be so, for all is contained within the Tree plan. To find the answer, we have to look at how the path structure originated.

To cut a long story short, there are twenty-two traditional paths for the simple reason that the Hebrew language has only twenty-two letters. Why Hebrew? Well, long ago when it was necessary to hide magical workings from the demon-possessed church, there had to be found a suitable written vehicle for knowledge. The only language beyond suspicion and yet of real value was Hebrew. Latin or Greek could not be used because priests could read and understand this without difficulty. Hebrew was not widely understood, yet for the simple reason that it was considered to be the biblical language, it was respectable and beyond suspicion—an ideal way in which to communicate ideas without attracting unwanted attention. The tradition of Hebrew is still with us, even though it has largely outlived its usefulness. Many people still attach great importance to Hebrew and thereby loose the reality of the Tree. Apart from making the Tree inflexible, there can be little sense in trying to speak and understand a language that is not your native tongue, other than for purely academic reasons.

If we take all the possible permutations of the known planets, we arrive at the true number of paths on the Tree of Life. This amounts to no less than fifty-five! However, while it is well to bear in mind that these paths do exist and, at some future date, you should begin to make a study of these, for the sake of convenience we will confine ourselves to using the accepted, traditional path arrangement. There are two good reasons for doing this. First, it keeps the number of options down to sensible proportions that the student can manage in the initial stages of magical work; second, it would serve no useful purpose to attempt to place all the paths onto the existing Tree design. To do this would simply serve to make the Tree virtually indecipherable. We will therefore stick to the traditional arrangement in this chapter.

By definition of the reality exposed by the movement of the planets in the heavens, a path is a link between planets, along which energy flows. It is the reality of the conjoined spheres as expressed through their union. A fair comparison would be the wire that connects two electrical components—without the wire, no power can flow and each component is therefore unable to fulfill its function. Spheres can exist without paths, but without the linking afforded by the paths, they are rendered inoperative. Such is the power of the paths. The lesson is simple. If you would seek the real power and potential of the Tree of Life, learn to understand the paths.

Like the spheres, each path has its own symbols and correspondences. There is only one set of attributions that is of any real value—the right ones! Although I may be belaboring a point, it cannot be stressed too strongly that most of the ideas, attributions, and symbols commonly associated with the paths, are absolutely useless. They stem from two main sources. First, the Order of the Golden Dawn and its devotees believed it and then presumed to inform everyone about their discovery. The attributions of the Golden Dawn are nonsense, in particular the colors and the tarot cards allotted to the paths. It is well known that this Order made certain that the truth of these matters was never revealed. This was particularly the case in the latter years when dogma and the need to throw sand in the eyes of neophytes became more important than helping them to find reality. In any case, quite a lot of these supposed attributions were arrived at using methods similar to those used by a trance medium. To say the least, they were unscientific and are best forgotten.

The reality of any path lies in the combined effect of the two spheres positioned at either end. From this simple truth we are able to build up a sensible set of meaningful attributions that will serve us well. Let us take, for instance, path eleven once more. This path joins sphere 1, Kether, with sphere 2, Chockmah. By looking at the physical level, the planets, we can deduce a great deal. First, the color of the path will be the combined color of the two planets. In short, it will be a combination of transparency and pure white. The best description is translucent white, and the nearest equivalent would be something similar to the effect obtained by diluting milk with water. Another way of doing this is to imagine that the colors do not completely mix so that one is suspended within the other—rather like globules of oil in water. All that matters is that you have some means of erecting this combination in your mind and, all things being equal, it does not matter what form this takes, as long as the idea of combination is adhered to. Use whatever suits you.

As further examples: Path thirteen, sphere 1, Kether, to sphere 6, Tiphereth, would be a mixture of transparency and gold, while path twenty-one, sphere 4, Chesed, to sphere 7, Netzach, would be turquoise (combined blue and green) or any of the variations of the two colors arrived at by using the ideas given previously. Paths to or from Malkuth can be a problem, for this sphere has four colors, those of the elements. This may be solved by using a rich brown to represent Malkuth.

Now let us turn our attention to the tarot. While the pedigree of the tarot is debatable, this does not impair its practical use. Versions of the Major Arcana featured in the ancient art of memory were associated with the Coptic, Greek Orthodox, and Roman Churches, where they remained, fragmented but recognizable, until recent injudicious modernization of liturgy and tradition. Whether denigrated by religious zealots as "the

Devil's picture gallery" or hailed by magical practitioners as the lost book of Thoth, the tarot's place in Magic remains assured. As the Minor Arcana cards fit the spheres, so the Major Arcana cards fit onto the paths. By far the best arrangement to date is that given by W. G. Gray in his notable books *Magical Ritual Methods* and *The Talking Tree.*[1] This arrangement is as follows.

PATH	SPHERES	TAROT TRUMPS
11	1—2	Heirophant
12	1—3	Hermit
13	1—6	Star
14	2—3	Judgment
15	2—4	Emperor
16	2—6	Temperance
17	3—5	Death
18	3—6	Hanged Man
19	4—5	Justice
20	4—6	Strength
21	4—7	Empress
22	5—6	Tower
23	5—8	Devil
24	6—7	Lovers
25	6—8	Chariot
26	6—9	Sun
27	7—8	Wheel of Fortune
28	7—9	High Priestess
29	7—10	World

[1] W.G. Gray, *Magical Ritual Methods* (York Beach, ME: Samuel Weiser, 1980); and, *The Talking Tree* (York Beach, ME: Samuel Weiser, 1977).

30	8—9	Magician
31	8—10	Fool
32	9—10	Moon

The tarot trumps, like the Minor Arcana cards, form an ideal focus for meditation or contemplation, either within a ritual framework or at odd moments when time permits. Naturally, knowing how the cards relate to the Tree of Life is bound to enhance your understanding of the cards in a way not possible to those who know nothing of this association.

The actual magical working of a path is a relatively simple affair, provided that you are familiar with the techniques for erecting the Cosmic Sphere and attuning this to a particular sphere. Without this knowledge, and lamentably this is the norm for most magical operators, pathworking is bound to be a laborious, unrelated experience, giving rise to much confusion, contradiction, and even wild speculation on the messages resulting from this lack of a cohesive base plan. At best, it will take years to discover anything worthwhile. At worse, it will simply add to the delusions of those who choose to carry on in an unscientific manner.

Each path is a combination of two spheres, so the logical approach must be one of erecting each sphere followed by an attunement to the path. Perhaps the easiest way to describe this is by actual example, so let us presume that the intention is to work the twenty-sixth path from sphere 6, Tiphereth, to sphere 9, Yesod. Here are some useful ideas that may be used or expanded on in your own way. They are for guidance only and are not to be taken as a rigid framework.

Step One—the Correspondences

Obviously, an entire range of altar cloths to cover each sphere and path would be extremely expensive to buy or time-consuming to make. A better solution is to have a plain white cloth and, if possible, vary this by using either colored cord or strips of cloth laid across the altar. In this case a gold cloth could be laid from left to right and a silver cloth laid from top to bottom.

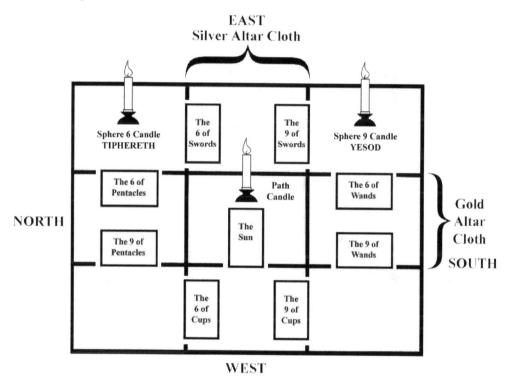

Figure 13. Altar Arrangement for Path Twenty-Six.

Use three candles, one for each sphere and one for the path. The sphere candles should be in the appropriate colors, while the path candle could be plain white. These may be lit at the appropriate time during the ritual and will therefore form a useful focus.

Use the all-important tarot cards. Place the major card representing the path—in this case the Major Arcana card, The Sun—in the center of the altar, being the main focus of attention, with the path candle directly behind it. In addition, use the Minor Arcana cards. As you face magical east, the 6 and 9 of Swords are placed to the east, the 6 and 9 of Wands are placed to the south, the 6 and 9 of Cups are placed to the west, and finally, the 6 and 9 of Pentacles are placed to the north. The sphere 6 (Tiphereth) candle is placed on the left and the sphere 9 (Yesod) candle is placed to the right. These may be placed on the altar or, if you prefer, on the appropriate quarters of the temple. Available space may well be the deciding factor in this matter. On page 135 is a diagram of an ideal altar arrangement for path twenty-six (figure 13).

I am often asked about incense for the path. Use either a combination of the sphere incenses or, alternatively, burn these separately in order that the natural mingling of the scents will produce the desired effect. There is no need to purchase specially made incense for each path.

Step Two—the Inner Work

The procedure for attuning the temple to a path is similar to that used with the spheres. Naturally, the temple would be opened using the now familiar techniques given in previous chapters. The main body of magical work now divides into three phases:

1. Attunement of the temple to the first sphere.
2. Attunement of the temple to the second sphere.
3. Final attunement to the path.

You will remember, from the previous chapters, that there are two distinct ways in which a sphere may be invoked—either objectively or subjectively. In order to change from one to the other, change the magical directions from natural to personal. Let us first consider the objective approach of working with the paths in an external manner.

In dealing with the paths, it is not important which sphere is invoked first; this is largely a question of personal choice. Let us presume that you are starting with sphere 6, Tiphereth. Direct attention to the Crown, see the gold jewel starting to glow, and then allow golden light to enter the temple in a clockwise direction, starting from magical south. Direct your attention to the lower point and the Cube. Again, this glows with the same light and is then allowed to enter the temple in a counterclockwise direction, once more starting at magical south. Light the candle representing this sphere as a symbolic indication that the temple is now open to Tiphereth and the Sun. If using separate incense, burn one now.

Next, invoke the second sphere, in this case sphere 9, Yesod. Again the same procedure: direct attention to the Crown, allowing the light to enter in a clockwise manner, starting with the correct magical direction, then direct your attention to the Cube and allow light to enter in a counterclockwise direction, and so forth. In this case, however, the light is silver and the magical direction is, of course, west. Again light the appropriate candle and burn the incense of the sphere. Finally, attune the temple to the path. There are several ways to do this, and with practice you will doubtless find others more in keeping with your own needs.

Keep matters as simple as possible in order not to burden the mind with complexities and confuse your subconscious. Imagine a doorway with the number of the path on it and/or the appropriate tarot trump. Pass through this door and explore the reality of whatever lies behind it, or simply allow impressions and ideas to arise in the mind. Naturally, this may once again be symbolized by the lightening of the path candle and the burning of incense.

Other possibilities include directing attention to the center and the inner cubic altar of gold. Alternate flashes of the path colors may be seen around this with, perhaps, the tarot trump lying on the top of the altar. From then on, it is simply a case of using the mind to explore this further by allowing impressions to rise up in the mind. There are many other possible variations and alternatives, and it is suggested that you think about these and then adopt that which appeals to you best, for the secret of successful Magic often lies in being contented with a particular way of working, rather than trying to "force" some idea to work. By all means use the ideas given in this book, but think about them, turn them over in your mind, and decide what is best for you.

Provided that you have carried out the procedure carefully, your mind will now be attuned to the correct path in a realistic manner. In short, your consciousness will have been narrowed down to one field of influence or tuned in to a selected band of awareness. At the end of the meditation, close down in the normal way. This may be given extra impetus by the extinguishing of the path and sphere candles. At conclusion, write up any notes for further consideration at a later date.

Having dealt with the subjective type of meditation, I should now point out that there is the objective (self) approach to be considered. In order to do this, one has simply to change the magical direction as described previously. You will find it interesting to compare results obtained from the two alternatives.

In the final chapter we will take matters considerably further by looking at your relationship with the cosmic tides and how you may use this to your advantage.

The Paths

The following list of path colors will prove to be useful. In certain instances, the sphere colors combine to form a further color (for example blue and yellow form green). This may be used instead of the more usual "oil and water" idea.

Path	Main Color	Alternative Color
11	Transparent/White	
12	Transparent/Black	
13	Transparent/Gold	
14	White/Black	Gray
15	White/Blue	
16	White/Gold	
17	Black/Red	
18	Black/Gold	
19	Blue/Red	Purple
20	Blue/Gold	Green
21	Blue/Green	Turquoise
22	Red/Gold	Orange
23	Red/Orange	Scarlet
24	Gold/Green	Lime Green
25	Gold/Orange	Amber
26	Gold/Silver	
27	Green/Orange	
28	Green/Silver	
29	Green/Brown	
30	Orange/Silver	
31	Orange/Brown	Russet
32	Silver/Brown	

The Cosmic Tides

In this final chapter we look at the spheres and paths in greater depth and attempt to show how you may vastly improve your work through the use of personal planetary attributions.

First we must return to the idea of polarity. It is evident throughout the cosmic scheme, for example Crown/Cube, east/west, north/south, center/periphery, and so on. It is also evident in everyday life; in fact, nothing would happen without polarity. We would have inertia. The study of polarity reveals much to the dedicated seeker, but for now, consider one aspect only—the polarity existing between you and life energies. By this we mean those energies that appear to be outside of the individual and are categorized under convenient headings, such as planetary or elemental.

Power and Symbolism

First realize that power flows freely from a creative source. This source is without form or direction and is unknowable in the normal sense. The Cabalistic Tree of Life recognizes this by referring to the Negative Veils. Esoteric writer W. G. Gray simplifies this by adding a zero sphere to the top of the Tree. However, what should be borne in mind is that this nothingness, this unknowable source of power, does exist and is the cause of the entire Tree. Trying to understand this source is impossible from a conscious point of view in that it is too abstract for the mind to grasp. Such are the difficulties encountered when dealing with this state of nonexistence.

In the realms of Practical Magic, whether the magician realizes this or not, he or she is giving form to the abstract source, which, in turn, pours its power into these thoughts. Sustain these thoughts and results are inevitable.

Humankind's ability to use the power of the creative source is beyond dispute—that is, unless one listens to restrictive dogmas such as those offered by religions. However, owing to the abstract nature of the source and the way in which this assists manifestation through human thoughts, various types of images have been used. God is one such image. The source lends power to images regardless of whether these images are good or bad, which accounts for the misery so evident in today's world. It is therefore vitally important to select images that are beneficial rather than self-restrictive. God, as such, is an image—nothing more. Lying behind any god-image is the eternal creative source from which true power emanates, and it is therefore a mistake to presume that God is power.

An individual's ability to contact and make use of the power of the source is made much easier through the use of images. Gods, archangels, angels, and the like are all convenient images for this very purpose. They are symbols. Likewise, the planets, elements, and the entire Tree of Life are also symbols by which creative power may be recognized and used. Put simply, they are specific images that, if used correctly in the mind, provide a channel for the flow of creative energy. For convenience, we adopt an attitude of mind that suggests that power is out there—it is objective. Most magical work uses this objective approach, but it is only part of the two-part equation.

Objective Power, Subjective Power, and Transiting Planets

One of the best ways of examining human potential is to use the birth chart. This is nothing more than a symbolic plan of a person's potential. It is not, as some would suggest, a map of destiny or a guide to karma.

These dogmas should be rejected by those who truly wish to know about Magic. Little work has been done on the purely esoteric implications found in such charts, which is a pity, for much can be gained in these matters. One such area of research is concerned with the discovery of a person's ruling planets. Apart from mundane uses, such as which planet rules, say, health in an individual's chart, there are obvious esoteric pointers.

Every planet in a birth chart is a symbolic point of contact with objective power, and much use of this is made in astrology. You have probably heard of astrological predictions through the use of transits and progressions. Put simply, this means that the astrologer calculates when a planet in the heavens is forming an aspect to a planet in your birth chart. From this, depending on the nature of both planets, certain trends may be deduced. Notice that I say *treads*. This is all that any astrologer can do. No one can predict with complete accuracy, for the simple reason that each individual has the right of free choice as to how he or she will use these energies. Prediction works because most people are predictable— not because karma, fate, or any other negative ideal takes control, but because most people choose to be so.

The planets in the heavens, known as transiting planets, are the symbolic pointers to specific types of creative energy. The planets in the birth chart, known as natal planets, are sensitive points that are symbolic of energy reception by the individual. Transiting planets are therefore objective power, natal planets are indicative of subjective power. The constantly changing relationship between transiting and natal planets is measured in terms of aspects. An aspect is simply a way of measuring when a transiting planet is capable of supplying its specific type of energy. These are measured in terms of angles. Some angles (such as 90°) are considered difficult, while others (such as 120°) are considered beneficial. However, the main point to remember is that when an aspect is formed, power flows from the creative source to a specific area of life. For instance, suppose we are dealing with a Jupiter transit to a natal Sun. The effect would be that Jupiter energy would flow and connect with the person's inner being, as symbolized by the Sun, the effect of which would work themselves out in terms of the combined effect of the two planets. One possibility would be an increase in optimism with perhaps a measure of good fortune. Of course, this is an oversimplification; there are many other factors to be considered. Nevertheless, the idea of a transit supplying the power to a receptive planet in the birth chart in correct.

What we must now consider is how to use this principle in a magical sense. When transit planets aspects natal planets, what does this tell us? In essence it shows that the polarity that exists between objective power (out there) and the receptive part of ourselves indicated by the subjective natal planet (within) is actually causing power to flow. If we look a little deeper, we will see that the flow of power, as indicated by the aspect, is clearly exhibited in the Tree of Life in the form of paths. What is a path other than the channel along which power flows between two spheres or two planets? Aspects therefore equate to paths of power.

Any planet is a symbolic indicator of a specific type of energy. It also corresponds to the Assiah level of a sphere. Now, consider this:

Objective Power: equates to the All-Father, positive part of a sphere. A planet in the heavens is indicative of this force.

Subjective Power: equates to the Earth-Mother, receptive part of a sphere and is symbolized by a planet in the birth chart.

Therefore, there are three possibilities:

1. Objective power, as indicated by the planets in the heavens, and their paths, as indicated by the forming of aspects to each other.

2. Subjective power, as indicated by the planets in the birth chart, together with similar paths formed by aspects.

3. Perhaps the most important is the combined effect of objective planets forming paths of power to subjective planets in the birth chart. Let us now consider what this means.

Esoteric Working
Involving Objective Power

In the first scheme, as the planets move around the solar system, they naturally form aspects, each aspect giving rise to a path of power. For instance, when the Sun aspects Mercury, path twenty-five (Tiphereth-Hod) is formed and the power flows. You will note that neither planet assumes the role of positive or negative; both are equal. Magically, this may be investigated by using the normal techniques given in the previous chapter on pathworking. An aspectarian may be used to determine when such paths are formed. [1]

Naturally, when as aspect is occurring in the heavens, the power is at peak and the resultant magical work is bound to be more effective than at any other time. It should be remembered that this does not mean that a particular path can only be worked when its equivalent aspect is formed in the heavens. Paths may be worked at any time but are likely to yield better results when an aspect exists.

---

[1] An astrological calendar can tell you when an aspect is exact or at its peak. https://horoscopes.astro-seek.com/monthly-astro-calendar

Esoteric Working
Involving Subjective Power

To use this technique you will need a copy of your birth chart. Either you can produce it yourself or one may be obtained from the many astrological services available.[2] Armed with this information, you are then in a prime position to investigate these paths from a personal point of view. Much may be learned about the self by using this technique. In this subjective approach, the personal magical directions are used throughout.

Pathworking

The third scheme brings together both objective and subjective modes of power and lends to true pathworking. There have been many attempts to portray pathworking, but most have been a copy of outmoded Golden Dawn ideas. The following scheme is beyond doubt the best available, for not only does it conform to sensible structure, it also takes account of what is happening in the heavens and how this relates to you. This type of pathworking has the advantage of linking together the positive, objective power of the heavens with the subjective part of yourself. It is the ulti-mate in polarity working.

The best way to illustrate this type of pathworking is by example. Let us suppose that you are about to work path twenty. This combines the

---

[2] *Zet 9* which is FREE software; you can generate interpretations for the lunar and solar transits, progressions of the planets or learn more about what the stars have reserved for you. *ZET Lite* is a feature-rich piece of software that enables you to create your natal chart, and make predictions about the events that can happen in the major sectors of your life. Also, *Time Nomad* is an astrology chart app for iPhone and iPad; charts for any location, natal charts, transits, synastry, progressions and planetary hour calculator. *Aquarius2Go* is a simple astrology app for Android which has an astrology chart application which features Zodiac chart for horoscope types: radix, transits, solar arc progression etc. Also, *TimePassages* for Android, your birth chart with interpretations, daily horoscope with personal transits, and up-to-the-minute current astrology.

spheres of Tiphereth and Chesed and the ruling planets the Sun and Jupiter. There are two way to do this. Either the power flows from sphere 6 to sphere 4, or the opposite. It is therefore necessary to determine beforehand which planet is to act in the positive, objective manner. For the sake of our example we will assume that sphere 6 is to act as the objective force while sphere 4 assumes the role of being receptive.

Attend to correspondences and other pre-ritual matters, and open the Inner Temple. Direct your attention first toward the objective sphere/planet by using the clockwise spiral of golden light from the Crown (gold being the color correspondence of sphere 6). See it enter the temple in a clockwise direction starting at magical south (the normal magical direction of the Sun). Allow this to build up in the imagination and, of course, make use of correspondences such as candles, incense, tarot cards, and so forth. The objective part of the equation is now complete.

Now you must bring in the subjective part. Turn your attention toward the base Cube, which is now to act as the symbol for the subjective force of Jupiter/Chesed. Imagine that this glows with blue light and that it rises upward in a counterclockwise direction. Because you are dealing with your own subjective planet, you must now use your personal magical direction as the point of entry into the temple rather than the normal direction (which, of course, equates to objective power). This will vary with different people. For the sake of our example, let us presume that your personal magical direction for Jupiter is east. Therefore, see the power enter the temple in a counterclockwise direction starting from magical east. Again, allow this to build up in your mind, bringing in appropriate correspondences and so forth. The remainder of the work will deal with the combined effect as given in previous chapters.

Do remember that a path can be worked at any time. However, if you know when these paths are actually being formed, these periods will most certainly lend weight to your efforts because you will be in tune with what is actually happening as decreed by the cosmic tides. The only way to know when these paths are formed is to have someone prepare an aspectarian showing when planetary transits are aspecting your natal planets. The alternative is to learn how to do this yourself. Any good book on astrology will help you with this.[3]

Although the greater part of this chapter has been devoted to paths, consider the spheres in their own right. These, also, may be worked from a polarity point of view using similar techniques. Up to now you have used only the objective approach, involving the natural magical direction of the planet. Let us now take this further.

As with the paths, there are three possible permutations:

1. Objective, using the planets in the heavens.

2. Subjective, using the planets in your birth chart.

3. Collective, which is a combination of objective and subjective planets.

Objective Planets

Deal with the reality of the power of the planet (and sphere) in its own right. Normal magical directions are used, for example, magical north for Venus and its ruling sphere Netzach. Sphere opening would consist of both clockwise and counterclockwise opening around this magical direction.

---

[3] Margaret Hone, *The Modern Textbook of Astrology* (London: L. N. Fowler & Co; 1951). Also, Yasmin Boland. *Astrology: A Guide to Understanding Your Birth Chart* (London, Hay House UK, 2016).

In dealing with the pure objective power of a single sphere, keep in mind that your work is with objective power. The normal magical direction applies; however, in more advance work you may choose to bring in the additional idea of the actual position of the planet/sphere in question. For example, if you were working with the objective power of the Sun, you would use magical direction south. If, at the time of working, the Sun was in, say, the sign of Taurus, then, by virtue of the fact that this is an Earth sign, solar power would also manifest through magical north.

Subjective Planets

These equate to the planets in your birth chart that are, of course, receptive in nature. In this case your personal magical directions apply, which may differ from the normal ones. Nevertheless, these specific directions should be used for this type of working.

Here we deal with fixed planets and aspects that can be meditated on and worked with from a personal point of view. In short, they are the best way to discover self. For this, turn to your personal planets. Two important points emerge. First, there is a natural linkage between a planet and its magical direction, for example, Mercury-Sword-magical east. This relates to the objective mode of power. In other words, the Magic Sword is the control symbol for the objective, positive power of Mercury and its sphere of Hod. Second, each weapon (and direction) also has a second rulership, which is determined by the planetary positions in your birth chart.

Let us suppose that your Magic Sword is ruling Venus. From a subjective point of view, Venus and its equivalent sphere of Netzach should be sought at the magical direction of east rather than at the traditional (objective) direction of north. Naturally, the Magic Sword will replace the Shield as control symbol. Such a working would consist of using both clockwise and counterclockwise temple openings around the personal magical direction. In case of confusion the rule is this:

For objective working, use the normal magical direction together with its appropriate control symbol.

For subjective working, use the personal magical direction with its appropriate control symbol.

Collective Workings

The Tree of Life is said to have thirty-two paths. This may seem a strange statement, yet it happens to be true if one considers the effects of polarity. For instance, it is a true fact that the Sun in the heavens must form aspects to the Sun in your birth chart, thereby forming a path. Add the ten paths so formed to the twenty-two traditional intersphere paths and we have a total of thirty-two. Think about this. A path between these planets is real and therefore workable.

Collective working of a planet/sphere is a simple affair that may be linked to actual aspects being formed in the heavens or, as always, may be done at any time. As with other schemes, better results are bound to occur when an actual aspect is formed due to peak energy flow. First direct attention toward the positive, objective planet and allow the power into the temple in a clockwise direction. Then direct your attention toward the subjective planet (which of course is the same), allowing this to enter the temple in a counterclockwise direction. Next, proceed as normal with your meditation.

Final Word

This book has been designed to help you build up a useful basis for growth and to give you lots of original ideas. The success or failure of the book depends on how much you are prepared to consider and apply these ideas. From now on it is up to you to continue with the work in your own way and at your own pace. Some additional information may prove to be of value.

You will come across many ideas, concepts, and ideals in your magical search. Never accept these as gospel or reject them out of hand. True knowledge is acquired by looking at everything coming within your awareness and then asking *why?* Question all. Remember that the path of true Magic lies in being an individual and only by questioning is this possible.

The sharing of experiences and knowledge is quite valid, provided that individuality is not sacrificed in favor of the herd instinct. It is one thing to join or perhaps form a group for mutual study or the accomplishment of a common aim, but it is another to be a slave to feelings of being left out or using the supposed comfort of a group to bolster a lack of self-confidence. Apart from groups, social esoterics has little to offer the serious student—these affairs are best left to the herd or those who are destined to be the puppets of whatever trend is in fashion.

Western minds must follow the Western path. This, in effect, means that you must look at the traditions of the West and adopt those that are meaningful. This is not an easy task, for much of our Western tradition has been buried under superstition or dogmatized by would-be priests, both past and present.

The real traditions are not necessarily found in lodges. In fact, I would be surprised if such organizations had any real insight into such matters. The real traditions are to be found in the land itself and can be contacted and worked with by anyone who has a will to do so. How, you may ask? The path is different for each soul. Ask and it will be given, seek and you will find, knock and it will be opened unto you. These are wise words. The key to the inner mysteries lies within you, within your subconscious mind. Seek to know and you will know.

Far too much emphasis is given to what are in effect pseudo-Eastern practices imported and capitalized on by those who have need of controlling masses of gullible people. The gullible seeker of occult knowledge can easily get mixed up with so-called Black Magic groups and find it difficult to get out due to threats. These groups so often either delude people or seek to rule by fear. That innocent cup of tea or glass of wine may well be spiced with something less tasteful or desirable and before you realize what is happening, you could be in a deep trance. In this condition it is quite easy to put suggestions into your mind to the effect that you will part with your money or be unable to say no to whatever requests are made of you. You do not think this can happen—it has and it still does! Hypnotism is widely used in the most subtle ways. In case you thought that you had to stare at bright lights or a swinging pendulum before you could be hypnotized you would be wrong. Often it is possible to talk someone into a trance, especially if mild herbal drugs have been administered to the wine or the incense. Of course there are other techniques of trance inducement and mind control techniques; some are used at initiations. The whole point is this: the lunatic fringes who indulge in this are not in any way, shape, or form interested in anything other than total domination for selfish reasons, and they will stop at nothing in order to have their own way. If normal fear techniques do not work, or pure lies do not work, then trance inducement is brought into play. Remember this: the type of people who look for masters or lodges of initiation are often gullible to begin with. This open-mindedness makes for easy access to those who know trance techniques, because the individual does not know what to expect and is often off guard. Also, you will find, as many others have found, that it is far easier to get *in* than it is to get *out*. Apart from fear there is evidence to suggest that certain factions use drugs, hypnosis, mind control techniques, and psychic attack (if you suspect psychic attack, remember with a resolute will any psychic attack will fail and, in any case those who are indulging in this sort of insanity will, sooner or later, reap their just rewards owing to the laws of cause and effect) to ensure that you stay loyal. You have been warned!

There is an ever-growing need for genuine organizations that will teach reality and sound techniques to all who are willing to learn. To this end these books I write offer a meaningful alternative to oppressive religions and/or supposed magical organizations who seek to fool others by perpetuating superstition, dogma, and unreality frequently peddled as occultism. It is common sense to look at other points of view and to compare the rites and traditions of other bodies of thought. However, to be deplored are the "get-rich-quick" or supposed "instant" Magic books which promise the earth yet, all too often, fail to get results. In short, you must find your own roots before you can hope to grow. Such roots are to be found in your native myths, customs, traditions, and practices. They are also evident in the ancient sites, not, as some would have you believe, in the form of trackways, but as a living, vibrant force that exists and has subtle effects on subconscious mind levels of awareness. Look to the land! Rediscover the folktales and ways of your ancestors and the Magic will come uninvited.

Finally, all forms of Magic are, in essence, practical. Ask yourself this: What is the point of a meditation if it does not give birth to a usable idea? Meditate, by all means, then act. These are not my words but the words of one who is truly wise. All too often the esoteric worker lives in a cloud-cuckoo land of unreality, presuming that his or her inner realizations are gifts or that they are sacred. This is nonsense. All that an esoteric worker can do is to extract from subconscious mind levels certain information that is likely to be of value to themselves or to the world in general. By all means keep personal information to yourself, but seek always to apply it. All great discoveries, inventions, and profound thoughts come from the subconscious mind. A thought, inspiration, or a flash of insight is nothing unless applied.

Look at the Tree of Life. Do you see its message? It is rooted in the good earth of Malkuth where it grows and bears fruit. No earth, no Tree—no Tree, no fruit. All must be rooted in earth before it can grow, and so it is with ideas. Also note that the power of the Tree descends to find fruition in Malkuth, yet another pointer to the reality of life and the need to give form to thoughts. Without thoughts there is no growth; nothing evolves in the truest sense of the word. Without earth there is no growth. Consider the analogy of trying to plant seeds without earth—it cannot be done. The power of thought, as indicated by the Tree, and the projection of these thoughts as actualities go hand in hand. They are inseparable. This is one of the real secrets of the Tree of Life. What will you harvest from its branches?

It is my sincere hope and wish that you, the student, find whatever you truly seek. If this book has in any way helped this cause, then I will be content; my work will be done. From now on the path is open to you. You will make mistakes and you will make discoveries. Both will help you rise above the norm of the herd-instinct mentality. Do not be afraid to explore new ground, and do not be afraid to think for yourself. You will make mistakes, but never forget that mistakes are the keys to greater things.

Magic is a science, the science of using the vast potential of the subconscious mind. Use it and it will transform your life. Use is well and you will *know*.

Appendix: Working with Telesmatic Images

Solomonic Magic can involve elaborate rituals to evoke a particular spirit or entity, and then summon it to appear in the Triangle of Art to do your bidding. However, before this can happen, you first need to get into a state of magical awareness where you are able to bring out these energies. Once evoked, you can communicate with these personalized energies, asking what you want of them and then sending then on their way to accomplish your desire.

When using Solomonic Magic, spirits are supposedly "summoned to appear," however, the appearance, more often than not is perceived in the mind of the magician or as a presence. The subconscious moves in mysterious ways and can manifest the most surprising phenomena, some of which appear to be objective—in other words "real." However, are they real or are they a believable manifestation of our mind? Personalized images, known as telesmatics, have a profound effect on the subconscious. God is a telesmatic, so are archangels, spirits and even demons. If we believe in these images then they apparently get results. The mistake is to believe that the image is an actual sentient being. The subconscious deals with images as a language so it tends to "speak back" in images. Again, it is important to remember that the image is not "real" even if this appears to be physical. It is a manifestation of the mind. Not everyone sees these manifestations, some people are more sensitive or aware than others, but for those who do it is essential to realize the place of such images in the greater scheme of things. Images have their use whether these are manufactured, or they simply appear to turn up at certain times providing that they are kept in perspective. The lesson is: use the image, don't let it use you.

Humankind has trifled with images for centuries without fully understanding what they were doing. Look at the classical image of God—it is man-made and pretty appalling into the bargain. Then again, "spirit guides" are easy to believe in—they are also the ultimate in self-deception. Images can lead to enlightenment or they can deceive—such is the power of an image.

External Entities, What are They?

Anyone new to the occult could well be excused for presuming that Magic is dangerous, or to say the least hazardous. Most people get involved with the occult through books and even movies, and so suitably armed with some grimoire they launch forth into the world of Magic armed with this so-called knowledge, presuming of course that the books cannot be wrong. In addition most people have formed an opinion of Magic which is likely to be wrong. The stories of Dennis Wheatley are certainly highly readable while movies like *Night of the Demon* are eerie little gems that you can enjoy with the lights off, but they have no relevance to what Magic is really all about.[1] From an occult point of view they serve to add to the superstition and fear which now surrounds occultism. Many supposed occult books do little other than add to the now familiar fear barrier so prevalent in today's magical circles. Rather than project common sense, they inevitably point out the fact that "something out there" is hell-bent on getting you, in fact this seems to be an obsession not based on reality that whatever it is that you seek—it can only be acquired if you deal with something "out there." Put simply there seem to be external entities to whom one must either grovel in order to

---

[1] A great film that focuses on the demonic occult; *Night of the Demon,* Sabre Film Productions, 1957. A British horror film, directed by Jacques Tourneur. It is adapted from the M. R. James story *Casting the Runes* (1911).

gain favor, or must try to allude in case they run rampant within the confines of your temple.

The entire concept of outside entities is quite wrong and is based on the supposition that these are in fact real. This is made because of a complete ignorance of the rules governing telesmatic images. A telesmatic image is a symbol—a personalized symbol to be used as a means of communication on inner levels, without going into great detail this type of image is in certain circumstances a far more effective way of contacting and understanding life's energy patterns and their purpose, for the simple reason that a correctly made image can be dealt with as though it were in actual fact *real*. It only appears to be real and it only exists in the mind of the magician who uses it. All manner of telesmatic images have been devised by past workers, some are now traditional like the Cabalistic gods, while others belong purely to individual worker's, however, the golden rule is, if you are going to use these images it is vital to realize that these things are the product of the mind. This is the problem with so-called demons—here we have a telesmatic image which has been deliberately made to represent some undesirable aspect of human nature, say for instance greed. Used properly the magician would use this as a focus in order to rid themself of greed. This is a perfectly valid technique of using negative imagery to obtain a positive result, however, a little knowledge being a dangerous thing, certain gullible people started to believe that demons really and truly existed and proceeded to tell others of this supposed truth. The net result being that generations of magicians now believe in demons as a reality even though this has absolutely no basis in fact, on the positive side we have just as much belief in the actual existence of angels and so forth, again without proof or as much as a second thought. The novice who has only the books, established tradition, or those who are supposed to be in the know to turn to will naturally make the same mistakes and continue to presume that there are indeed external entities controlling occult matters, unless someone reveals the truth. Up to now that truth has been buried under heaps of superstition by those who should know better, however, you have at least been given the facts in the hope that a new and better tradition will evolve.

Magical Awareness and Ritual Magic

All magical work needs an atmosphere of calm and tranquility, the more you can turn off the conscious mind and allow the subconscious to take over the better, and this cannot be done if there is a constant fear of interruption. The whole idea to a ritual is to close your mind from mundane everyday affairs and to allow the subconscious to work. In magical practice it is essential that the mind be clear of all but the intention. Magic is done on a subconscious level and the reasoning logical mind, cluttered and clouded as it is with everyday events invariably gets in the way. Pre-ritual relaxation leaves the mind calm with a clear channel to the subconscious, and with regular practice you will reach the desired state of magical consciousness. If you do not connect to the subconscious then you have simply wasted a lot of time, energy and money on what amounts to no more than theatricals. The power of Magic lives in your own mind.

The reason that some rituals are long and drawn out is not to concentrate power for the entire time, any ritual is used to build up to the peak of magical awareness, to gradually quite the mind and reach a level of consciousness useful for some magical activity. By starting at the mundane level, each step of consciousness modification is achieved by an action—the lightening of a candle, the burning of incense, an anointing, an invocation, and so forth.

The way I invoke a planetary energy is purely through the telesmatic images of the archangels. I rarely do Practical Magic rituals anymore, which is rather odd because I could do more to help my material situation and reach my personal and magical goals. I suppose it is very strange not to be commanding my angels to go off into the world and bring me back some pennies now and again. However, when you get really heavy with the esoteric side of Magic, the practical side of it really, truly seems mundane. It cannot be explained; it is like when you just know something you cannot explain! I have had such fantastic experiences on the Tree, and it is just not possible to describe it. If you do a practical ritual, you will get practical results, but there is nothing happening inside, on the other levels. With esoteric rituals there is an enormous sense of fulfillment, joy, love, and a serenity that stays with you. At the climax of these rites, the intense purity and beauty and power of feeling is just— incomprehensible.

Getting to Know the Archangels

I had pictures in my mind of how the archangels should look from reading *The Ladder of Lights,* by W.G. Gray, and so my journeys on the Tree incorporated these pictures into my visualizations. It is hard work, but it does not take long before they hear your call and recognize your work.[2] The way I perceive Jupiter, I expected Tzadkiel to be a well-rounded, jolly, middle-aged type, but when he decided to make an appearance, Tzadkiel was really rather smallish, quite young, and had an Egyptian hair-style and robes with rather Latin features. So you cannot really go about it with preconceived ideas!

Make no mistake—telesmatic entities are within you. One day, a friend gave me a phone number of a clairvoyant. "Go and see her. She is brilliant!" my friend said. I phoned this lady, who would only let me tell her my name. She knew nothing else about me. She only knew my friend

---

[2] W. G. Gray, *The Ladder of Lights* (York Beach, ME: Samuel Weiser, 1981).

through her services. The night before I went to see her I decided to travel up to Tiphereth and get some sunny advice from the archangel Michael. I could not believe it the following day when he came through at my sitting with this lady. He wanted to be sure I knew who he was, and she said, "He is bringing you the Star of David." Whimsy, you think? Then you are still unaware of reality, for everything about you, including yourself, is a vehicle for divine intelligence. I was really thrilled about this. It proved to me that my work on the Tree was actually doing something. You have to be patient, settle down, be persistent, and develop your own system from the basic information given in this book and from *The Ladder of Lights*.

I will give you an example of a Tiphereth ritual. (It is good to start at Tiphereth because it is the sphere of self).

Working the Tree Plan

I only use incense and some music if I am working on a Practical Magic ritual (unless I am working within Malkuth on the Tree of Life). Because the Tree of Life rituals are quite involved, I use the necessary aids. I do not feel the need to dress for a ritual. Dressing up is rather like preparing to put on a performance, which goes against what I try to do in a rite. I am not ridiculing robes, for the idea behind them is sound. They do make you feel different, and I suppose a robe could be imbued with the wear's power so that when it is worn it enhances that power. I, however, feel different enough during ritual, even without a robe; it is a state of mind.

The Preparation

Once I know what rite I will be doing next, I fix a date for it. Prior to the date, I think about the rite, mentally rehearse it, and study that sphere so when the time arrives, I am totally psyched.

As I said, I do use all the necessary aids, and I suppose I use very little by comparison. When the time arrives, I always have a bath. I view it as a ritual, a means of change. Whatever you want, be it physical, mental, or spiritual, a change in personality, circumstances, fortunes, knowledge, or whatever. It is a want for something. By having a bath, (a) I get relaxed so my mind can settle and think about the next hour or so, get the rite in focus, and mentally rehearse it for the last time, and (b) I wash away the negative obstacles, cleanse them from my system, so when that plug is pulled, the obstacles go down to the sewer with the rest of the grime. If a bath is impossible (for example on a train or somewhere) the old Yogic practice of breathing in the positive and breathing out the negative is very effective.[3]

On to the rite. I lock the door and jam the door bell, unplug the phone and set my cell phone to silent, then go to wherever I have decided I am going to be on this occasion to perform the rite. I will have laid everything out before I got in the bath: The appropriate tarot cards at the quarters, a candle of the correct color, a bowl of dark liquid, (Guinness is good, when left to go flat and lose its froth, is ideal for scrying) the correct incense for the rite, and some appropriate music I have prepared earlier for the occasion on my MP3 sound station.[4]

I decided to start at Tiphereth and go straight to the heart of the Tree. I brought a gold piece of mounting board on which I drew two concentric circles and a dot in the center, from which I emanate. Then I put in my Equal-Armed Cross. I decide that inside the circles is my own Malkuth,

---

[3] Even washing your hands can symbolize a cleansing of the negative. Pontius Pilate did this at Christ's trial, and today healers do it.

[4] *Five Elements: Wind, Earth, Water, Fire and Space Meditation Music* by Global Mantra Music. Also, new age ambient, meditation, and Reiki etc. The world's best selling new age music, relaxation and ambient music label. https://newworldmusic.com

my Inner Temple, but I do not want to be confined to Malkuth, so I draw in the four gateways at the outer points of the circles.

I place the appropriate tarot cards (the four 6s) at the correct quarters, and place in the center a card that I feel represents what I am trying to do. My bowl is placed where I can gaze into it. I light the candle before I get into the bath and light the incense once I have started the ritual. I spend some time, before I begin, concentrating on the intention, even if this means writing it all down or speaking it aloud. Whatever it takes. Then I carry on with the rite as usual.

I have found that getting through the ritual quite quickly (without rushing) is the best solution. No one can concentrate for long periods of time. If you practice getting through rites quickly, the subconscious will get use to it. Spend extra time concentrating on the intention, but the quality of concentration is more important than the length of time put in. If you need to use extra aids, use them—if it's a person, use an image doll; if it is money, use a coin. Use whatever comes to mind. Who cares what it is? Who is going to know? It is only a matter of getting into a habit, finding a formula that works for you.

I have different plans for all the different spheres and keep them like separate entities. It is important to contact and make friends with the archangels. W. G. Gray gives sort of basic personalities for all of them. All these different personalities have different jobs to do. Learning about them all sets the imagination on fire, and all magical work thrives on imagination. When the imagination is fired up, it is easier to feel, especially if you begin to know these telesmatic entities and adopt some sort of feeling for them. Believe in them totally on the one hand, but remember they are only telesmatic forms of energy.

Get a copy of *The Ladder of Lights,* by W. G. Gray, and learn about the energies *before* you incorporate them. Below is a copy of a plan I use from my very own notebook. I had thought that all the rituals would be exactly the same, as the basic plan would be the same for all of them. I could not have been more wrong. Every ritual is completely different, which, for a start, proved to me that all these energies really do have different personalities. I hope my long-winded illustrations make the point clearly. I do not think you could make friends with a sphere, but the telesmatic from that sphere? Certainly.

Basic Ritual for Spheres on the Tree of Life Using Telesmatic Images

Type: Tiphereth

Drawn on gold card.

Clockwise indicates receptivity, counterclockwise for meditations, instructions, and so forth. First, acknowledge Gabriel: (west). Standing before you, he is dressed in long, flowing robes of blue and mauve hues that flash and shimmer; he wears a silver breastplate emblazoned with a trumpet, his face is of iridescent pearl, and he has very deep-set facial features. He holds a silver Chalice in the air and he is surrounded by water. The Chalice overflows with a blue liquid. Gabriel is archangel of the Water element. Imagine him clearly standing before you. Imagine behind him the coolness of the evening and a far-off sea shore with the waves rolling gently over the golden sand and the sound of seagulls calling to each other. As you do, sense the feeling of water surrounding you. Spend some time on this image. Then let go of the image and take a half turn to your right so that you are facing the archangel Auriel.

Secondly acknowledge Auriel: (north). He is dressed in the colors of Nature, for he is the archangel of the element of Earth. His long robes are emerald green, olive citrine, russet with flecks of black. He wears a copper breastplate emblazoned with sheaves of corn and in his hand is a Shield of intricate design, which represents the Earth element. Imagine him standing clearly before you. Imagine behind him a night sky filled with shining stars. A bright crescent Moon shines down. Sense the feeling of standing on earth, smell the moist earth, and be one with the earth. Let go of this image and turn another half turn so that you are facing the archangel Raphael.

Thirdly, acknowledge Raphael: (east). Standing there before you, he is dressed in yellow-orange. He wears a knee-length, short-sleeved tunic of golden ochre. In his hand is a large Sword, and on his bronze breastplate and cloak is the symbol of the Caduceus, the symbol is a double helix, a short staff entwined by two serpents, sometimes surmounted by wings. Raphael is the archangel of the Air element. Imagine him standing before you. Imagine behind him a beautiful sunrise in which the welcoming rays of the Sun is bringing the Earth to life. Sense the feeling of blowing air. Once again, spend some time on this, and then let go of the image and make another half turn to the right so that you are facing the archangel Michael.

Finally, acknowledge Michael: (south). Standing before you, he is dressed in golden armor of which no weapon made can penetrate it and a cloak with the colors of fire—flaming red with vivid flashes of orange. His hair is auburn, and he wears a breastplate emblazoned with a Lion's head. In his hand he carries a flaming Spear. Michael rules the Fire element. Imagine behind him a warm summer day with the Sun high in a cloudless sky, shining brightly. Sense the heat and the feeling of the gold flames of fire which lick the ground beneath his feet. With the inspiration of the archangels, erect the Triple Rings and enter your Inner Temple in preparation for your journey through Tiphereth.

After the sphere erection, go through the door of Assiah in the Inner Temple and focus your attention at the pool on your intention. Relax and keep aim in focus and see if anything appears. Move then toward the door of Yetzirah. See if a symbol appears, go through the door. What is happening? Notice the work force (or Malakim) inside doing their work.

Move through slowly and see what is going on. Then comes the door of Briah; see if a symbol appears, go through the door. Michael is warm and friendly. See what is going on in his world. Then move toward the door of Atziluth and observe Michael issuing orders to the Malakim. Knock on the door. Any symbols appearing? We all go in and enter the realm of the Sun's center. Look around, note anything important. We come face to face with the Eloah va Daath. We tell him everything we want to tell him. Listen for replies. Observe him giving orders to Michael. We bow and leave. We go through Michael's realm. We drop off the Malakim on the way. Michael instructs them. Michael and I again enter Assiah, where Michael leaves me to come back to my own mundane world.

Bibliography

Boland, Yasmin. *Astrology: A Guide to Understanding Your Birth Chart.* London, Hay House UK, 2016.

Bunning, Joan. *Learning the Tarot: A Tarot Book for Beginners.* York Beach, ME: Samuel Weiser, 1998.

Cooper, Phillip. *The Magickian: A Study in Effective Magick.* Northampton, England: Magickmeister, 2021.

_____. *Basic Magick: A Practical Guide.* Northampton, England: Magickmeister, 2021.

_____. *Secrets of Creative Visualization.* Northampton, England: Magickmeister, 2021.

_____. *Teach Yourself Tarot: The Quick & Easy Way.* Northampton, England: Magickmeister, 2019.

Crowley, Aleister. *777 and Other Qabalistic Writings.* York Beach, ME: Samuel Weiser, 1999.

Cunningham, Scott. *The Magic of Incense, Oils and Brews.* St. Paul, MN: Llewellyn, 1987.

Gayley, Charles M. *Classic Myths in English Literature.* Boston, MA: Ginn & Company, 1893.

Gray, William G. *Inner Traditions of Magic.* York Beach, ME: Samuel Weiser, 1978.

_____. *Magical Ritual Methods.* York Beach, ME: Samuel Weiser, 1980.

_____. *The Ladder of Lights.* York Beach, ME: Red Wheel/Weiser, 1982.

_____. *The Talking Tree.* Cheltenham, England: Skylight Press, 2014.

Hone, Margaret. *The Modern Textbook of Astrology*. London: L. N. Fowler, 1951.

Ophiel. *The Art and Practice of Clairvoyance*. York Beach, ME: Samuel Weiser, 1969.

_____. *The Art and Practice of the Occult*. York Beach, ME: Samuel Weiser, 1976.

_____. *The Art and Practice of Contacting the Demiurge*. Oakland, CA: Peach Publications, 1978.

Schueler, Gerald J. *Enochian Physics: The Structure of the Magical Universe*. St Paul, MN: Llewellyn, 1988.

Smith, Steven, *Wylundt's Book of Incense: A Magical Primer*. York Beach, ME: Samuel Weiser, 1989

Taylor, Maxine. *Now That I've Cast It, What Do I Do With It?* (MaxineTaylor.com) Independently published, 1975.

Vinci, Leo. *Incense: Its Ritual Significance, Use, and Preparation*. New York, NY: Samuel Weiser, 1980.

Index

Other Magickmeister Titles

Liber Abr
The Philosophy and
Principles of Magick
Phillip Cooper
ISBN 978-1-7399019-0-5

Liber Abr is a Magickal training course. Included is the ritual of Abramelin, (modern version) and Luciferian alchemy; also covered are the correct incense recipes, self-initiation, making a Magickal oath and astral Magick.

Teach Yourself Tarot
The Quick and Easy Way
Phillip Cooper
ISBN 978-1-7399019-3-6

The easy-to-read style makes it a wonderful introduction to tarot and the perfect spiritual tool for meditation and daily advice. It is a thoroughly tested, reliable and user-friendly self-study program for those who want to do tarot readings for themselves and others.

Basic Magick
A Practical Guide
Phillip Cooper
ISBN 978-1-7399019-6-7

He provides instruction for using the Inner Temple, building a Magick circle, working with four gateways of power, creating servitors and achieving Magickal trance. He also includes a complete discussion of planetary energy. In easy-to-understand terms, you learn what Magick is and what it can do to enhance your life. Whether you are a novice or seasoned practitioner, this step-by-step guide shows how to make Magick work!

Basic Candle Magick
An Easy to Follow and
Highly Practical Guide
Phillip Cooper
ISBN 978-1-7399019-5-0

This book presents the facts as they really are and helps you succeed in bringing happiness and fulfillment into your life through the use of natural energies. The accent is on simplicity, common sense and the use of practical candle burning techniques to get positive results.

Made in the USA
Middletown, DE
20 July 2024

57760667R00111